Towards a science
of science teaching

Towards a science of science teaching

Cognitive development and curriculum demand

Michael Shayer and Philip Adey

 HEINEMANN EDUCATIONAL BOOKS

Heinemann Educational Books
22 Bedford Square, London WC1B 3HH

LONDON EDINBURGH MELBOURNE AUCKLAND
HONG KONG SINGAPORE KUALA LUMPUR NEW DELHI
IBADAN NAIROBI JOHANNESBURG
EXETER (NH) KINGSTON PORT OF SPAIN

ISBN 435 57825 1

Typeset by Red Lion Setters, London WC1
Printed and bound in Great Britain by
Richard Clay (The Chaucer Press) Ltd
Bungay, Suffolk

Preface

Every day in school laboratories children are being asked to use the thinking skills of scientists. They are expected to classify objects, to control variables, to estimate chance, and to think of possible combinations of elements. How reasonable is it of us to make such demands? It may seem difficult to answer this question without more detail about what is meant by 'classify', 'control', and the others, but it is the daily experience of many science teachers that the demands are unreasonable, that there is a chasm set between the expectations expressed in curriculum objectives and the cognitive skills of many pupils.

This problem has been accentuated by the trend towards establishing science as an essential part of the educational experience of *all* pupils. The teaching of science has in all countries, until quite recently, been confined to an elite corps of teachers for an elite of pupils. Bloom (midwife to the famous *Taxonomy*) put the proportion of pupils whom the system was really interested in as low as 5 per cent. Now science is thought to be suitable and desirable for all children in primary and secondary schools [18]. Recent (1978, 1980) reports from the Inspectorate on primary and secondary schools in England and Wales, and the Association for Science Education's policy discussion document [1] all assume the principle of 'science for all'. What changes are necessary in the tradition of science teaching, especially in secondary schools, to suit it for this new role? How can teachers choose activities which match their pupils' powers to understand them? How can they evaluate their choice, and most quickly modify their curricula in the light of that evaluation? These are the questions towards which this book is directed.

The ideas and results presented here could be expected to have a wide range of application, since they introduce a way of thinking about secondary school problems, such as that of mixed ability teaching, which any teacher might find helpful. But the book is addressed firstly to science teachers. In effect, we attempt to turn around our training as scientists to develop ways of thinking about the teaching of science, and also ways of adding to that thought. It is the nature of scientific thought that it not only gives knowledge, but is progressive in that the exercise of scientific knowledge tends to produce fresh knowledge. It is partly on these grounds that time spent on it in schools can be justified. Science is one of the modes of experience, and it is an important one. It is just because it is so important that the ability of children to understand it, each in his or her own way, must be considered. One of the main arguments of this book is that there is a massive mismatch in secondary schools between the expectations institutionalised in courses, textbooks, and examinations and the ability of children to assimilate the experiences they are given.

Now we cannot expect science teachers to accept such a view without being given the evidence which they can judge according to the standards of their own training. Thus a substantial portion of this book is a presentation of the research which lies behind the conclusions reported, research which has grown out of the science work of the Concepts in Secondary Mathematics and Science Programme (CSMS). CSMS was established at the Chelsea College Centre for Science Education in 1974 with a grant from the Social Science Research Council for two full-time workers in science and three in mathematics for five years. The task taken on by the science side of CSMS was to investigate childrens' difficulties in science, by applying a Piagetian model of cognitive development to the practice of science teaching. The programme included

- some fundamental work to validate the Piagetian model;
- a large scale survey of middle and secondary school pupils to establish typical levels of thinking skills; and
- the development of a method for assessing the level of demand made on pupils by science curriculum activities.

Some conclusions which must follow from the results may be profoundly disturbing for science teachers, teacher educators, and others involved in science education. We do not believe, however, that they need be unduly depressing, since the instruments of measurement and analysis that we describe contain in themselves the promise of new methods of improving the quality of science education. The instruments highlight current deficiencies, but they also provide the tools by which such deficiencies may be rectified.

The book is divided into four parts. Part 1 (Chapters 1 & 2) introduces the problem and provides an overview of the methods used and the results obtained. Part 2 (Chapters 3 to 7) gives more detail of the Piagetian framework of the research, and of the design, construction and use of the class tasks developed for assessing levels of cognitive development. Part 3 (Chapters 8 to 10) introduces and provides details of the taxonomies developed for assessing the demand level of curriculum material, including studies checking on the validity of the taxonomies. Part 4 (Chapters 11 to 13) discusses the implications of the results presented in Parts 2 and 3, detailing the extent of the mismatch between curriculum and pupil population, indicating strategies for improving the match, and considering the nature of the possible new science curricula of the eighties and nineties.

The non-specialist reader may prefer to read first Parts 1 and 4, which contain the essential points we are making. Part 3 is designed for more prolonged study and provides a method by which the science teacher can analyse the level of thinking required for the comprehension of lesson objectives without needing to study the works of Piaget. Part 2 links the method of Part 3 to the Piagetian framework implied, and both these parts detail the extent to which the findings presented have been arrived at by a process of research which is scientific.

January 1981

Michael Shayer
Philip Adey

Acknowledgements

The research on which this book is based was funded by the SSRC on grant no. HR2693, Concepts in Secondary Mathematics and Science, and we thank them and the initial directors of the programme at Chelsea College, Kevin Keohane and Geoffrey Mathews, for their support. We also thank Kenneth Lovell for his sympathetic and wise advice, particularly in the earlier phase of the research. Since he became Director of the Centre for Science Education at Chelsea College, Paul Black has maintained a critical but involved interest in the programme. In the conduct of the work itself Hugh Wylam, a full-time member of the CSMS team, played a major role, especially in the development of the class tasks (Chapter 4) and in the work on Heat concepts described in Chapter 6. Jill Sutcliffe provided valuable assistance particularly in respect of biological concepts. We are grateful to all of these.

We thank also nearly fourteen thousand pupils with whom we have been directly or indirectly involved in the course of research, and who have nearly always suffered us gladly. We are equally grateful to some four hundred teachers who have given time to making arrangements for us, and in most cases taken some active part in the research. Ann Squires, from the Education Department of the City of Leeds, has given us invaluable help in contacting teachers in middle schools. We single out also (in Chapter 8) those persons who were on the consultative committee since they became, for the time, our partners in the work of developing the curriculum analysing taxonomy. In addition, Jeff Moore carried out much of the data-analysis on which Chapter 10 is based.

If the methods described in this book are seen to be sound and thorough, a fair measure of the credit must go to those people mentioned above. But if you wish to argue about the underlying philosophy of the research, or the conclusions we draw, then you must argue with the authors.

We acknowledge also:

Routledge and Kegan Paul for permission to reproduce quotations used in Chapter 3, from *The Growth of Logical Thinking*, by Inhelder and Piaget. The current edition is the second impression of 1967, but our quotations were taken from the 1958 first edition.

NFER Publishing Company, from whose *Science Reasoning Tasks, General Handbook*, Table 4.1 is taken.

Academic Press, for Figure 12.1 which was printed in Epstein, *Development of Brain Size* (1979).

Education in Chemistry, for Figure 2.3.

School Science Review, for Figure 2.4 and 2.5.

Contents

Part 1

Part 1

1 Looking for a model

The problem that we propose to address is that of the difficulty that many children find with learning science in secondary school. It is not necessary to rehearse the arguments for the vital role of science in education to see this as a problem worthy of serious investigation, but what methods are available for such an investigation? One approach might be to take particular concepts such as equilibrium, or ecology, or power, and to analyse the sub-concepts or bits of knowledge that are their prerequisites. Maybe in these prerequisites, or in the relationships between them, a particular source of difficulty will be identified which can be given more time, or restructured so that the approach to the main concept is made easier. This is a method that has been used to good effect in tertiary education and with selective secondary school curricula.

A problem with this approach is that it deals with the curriculum in a piecemeal fashion, one concept at a time, which makes it rather laborious and inefficient. Far more seriously, such a purely empirical attack on the problem does not help to build up any general theory of matching material to pupil. In this sense it is an unscientific approach, consisting as it does of observation and description, but omitting the critical phase of generalisation. If we are to make useful progress in our investigation into the nature of children's difficulties, economy demands that we seek some *model* of learning processes which can be applied generally over a wide range of individual learning experiences. A model of atmospheric behaviour allows us to predict, given certain data of pressures, temperatures, and dates, that it will rain in Manchester this Saturday afternoon. A model of catalytic action allows a chemist to predict the *sort* of compound that is likely to promote the oxidation of pollutants in a car's exhaust. The predictions may be far from certain, but they are very much better than chance, and they do help to direct our actions (take a raincoat to the City-United match, or select for trial a dozen or two out of the millions of possible potential catalysts).

The purpose of scientific model-building is not so much to satisfy curiosity about how things work (although that can be very useful) as to increase the chance of making accurate predictions which allow one to take action purposefully rather than at random, and so gain some control. Without a more general model of learning one can only accumulate books full of pyramids of problems based on patterns based on concepts based on knowledge [48] and yet remain unable to say that '*this* child will not be able to assimilate *that* concept at *that* level, but she will, given the right teaching conditions, be able to comprehend it at *this* level'. In other words, we need a model so that we can predict success and failure, not necessarily with one hundred per cent accuracy, but enough to increase significantly the chance of getting the child-material match right. With such predictive ability we can describe some of the limits within which the curriculum must be set for a given pupil, group, or population.

What sort of model?

Let us try to describe some features of a model that will help us to get inside the problem that we are set.

There are two major aspects to the difficulties that children have with learning science. There is the curriculum, which includes the concepts and skills to be taught and the method of teaching them; and there is the group of children to whom the material is to be taught. Things to be learned, and learners: the dichotomy is so obvious that it hardly seems worth making. And yet if you are looking for a model of learning that will usefully direct your investigations you must keep both of these aspects clearly in view, and strenuously resist the temptation to take up with models, however elegant, that place undue emphasis on one at the expense of the other.

There are, for instance, the ideas of structuring learning material developed by psychologists such as Gagné and Ausubel. These are without doubt valuable guides to teachers and curriculum writers who know what concepts have to be taught, and at what level, and who are struggling with the problem of arranging sub-concepts or the prerequisite bits of knowledge in the order which will most effectively promote learning. In particular the subtlety of the Ausubelian ideas on curriculum organisation will commend themselves to anyone who has puzzled over the best way to introduce complex concepts, such as the periodic table to fifth form (grade 11) chemists, or genetics to sixth form (grade 12) biologists.

But such ideas about the arrangement of learning material do not say enough about the child. Ausubel's famous plea 'to start from what the learner already knows' leaves unanswered the question about how one can describe or measure what the learner knows, and more importantly, what processing skills the learner has available to cope with new material. It is perhaps for this very reason that models which concentrate on the learning material (or to widen the context, on the whole learning environment) are so popular, especially among those who have some moral or political objection to 'labelling children'. By blaming all learning difficulties on the material, we can avoid the embarrassment of having to say that one child processes information faster or more efficiently than another. In this book, and in the science work of the CSMS programme, we take the view that such a position is untenable by anyone who chooses to consider the evidence with a scientist's eye, rather than with a politically blinkered one.

To review the argument so far: it is being maintained that

(a) nothing less than a general model of learning will enable us usefully to predict likely success and failure in the school laboratory, and
(b) the model must address with equal power both the learning material and the pupils' thinking processes.

In our search for a model to help us select or develop learning material suitable for a given group of pupils, we choose to restrict ourselves to the cognitive domain. This is not to say that considerations of motivation, interest, relevance, physical facilities, and motor skills are unimportant. But we do see cognitive matching as imposing the first of the set of limits within which new curriculum material must be set.

Piaget revisited

The major concern of Jean Piaget and his co-workers, the primary objective of their work, has been to try to elucidate the nature of knowledge. How is it that knowledge is structured? Can all concepts be reduced to simple bits of information or are there natural 'hard nuts'? Since knowledge and the person that knows are so closely connected, it seems proper to study the former by looking at the way that it is assimilated by the latter. Piaget's first intention in interviewing children was to develop a theory of the structure of knowledge, rather than a theory of the structure of the mind. The theory built on a lifetime of observations of children from birth to 16 years old is essentially a theory about the development of cognition in children, rather than about the development of children.

There is necessarily an intimate link between the structure of knowledge and the mental structure of one who knows. If Piaget has established that there is growth in the child's ability to perceive, process, and use data, then this implies a hierarchy of complexity in the possible ways that data may be processed. This in turn suggests a hierarchy of levels of comprehension asked for by a set of learning materials. The powerful attraction of the Piagetian model for the present purpose is that it should be possible to develop from it two sorts of measuring instruments:

1 for measuring the level of development of pupils' mental schemas,
2 for determining the level of cognitive complexity of curriculum material.

If both of these measures are made on the basis of the same set of postulates, then logically it should be possible to determine the upper limit of the level of curriculum material that can be handled by each pupil or group of pupils.

This, then, is the promise offered by the Piagetian model: a promise that no other learning theory could offer, and one that was allowed to guide, but not to direct, the course of our investigations. The distinction between guidance and direction is important. A guide is one who is in your employ, to whom you can say 'I think we will climb that mountain this morning', and then half way up change your mind and go back to the pub. A director chooses the mountains and the routes up them, and allows no diversions however shaky one's faith becomes in him. The scientist uses a theoretical model as a guide, that is, he goes along with it as long as it yields results which are useful, or as long as it continues to lead him into fruitful new areas of investigation. When the fruit dries up, or when the model has to be unreasonably strained to fit reality, then it must be abandoned or modified. Thus we accepted the model of Piaget, but with a measure of scepticism, and a willingness to use only those parts which could be validated to our own satisfaction.

An aspect of the model that we certainly cannot ignore is the idea of stages of development. Stage theory is central to the Piagetian world view, and is its most distinctive feature. According to this theory, the way that a child thinks develops through distinct stages as he/she grows up. The quality of thinking, the actual method of processing data received through the senses, is different at different stages. Piaget talks of mental structures characteristic of each stage which may be seen as processors, or systems which deal with incoming messages. The way that they do this, and the complexity of information that can be processed, will depend on the complexity of the mental structures.

In secondary school populations we can identify two major types of thinking. Younger and less able pupils will be limited to the use of *concrete operational* thinking, while older and more able pupils will have available a facility to handle abstractions and many-variable problems which is a characteristic of *formal operations*. Each of these stages may be divided into early and late phases, and we will use the following notation to indicate stages and substages from pre-operational to late formal operational thinking:

1 pre-operational
2A early concrete operational
2B late concrete operational
2B/3A transitional
3A early formal operational
3B late formal operational.

Single paragraph descriptions of pre-operational, concrete operational, and formal operational thinking generally serve to confuse the reader innocent of Piagetian psychology, and to infuriate the cognoscenti by their inadequacy. Later we will offer some validation for stage theory, and fill in many of the characteristics of formal and concrete stages derived both from Piaget's observations and from our own.

For now, armed only with the names of the stages, and the idea that generally a child who displays concrete operational thinking with respect to one topic will also do so when faced with other topics, we will proceed to an overview of the use we have made of the Piagetian model in the CSMS programme.

2 Applying the model

Population surveys

Firstly, we have developed a way of assessing stages of cognitive development of pupils in class groups of 25 or more at a time. Details of the development of the unique instruments, called **Science Reasoning Tasks**, necessary for this survey will be given in the second section of this book. Here we will summarise the results of a survey of a representative sample of the school population of England and Wales. Some 12 000 pupils from middle, comprehensive, and selective schools were assessed. Every child completed at least two tasks, sampling different aspects of behaviour characteristic of each stage of cognition. As would be expected from the stage theory of cognitive growth, agreement between any two tasks as to the operational level of a child was generally good (see Chapter 7). The mean level from the two tasks is used in presenting the results here.

Figure 2.1 shows, for a representative sample of the school population of England and Wales, the proportion of children at each age from 9 to 16 years (the statutory school leaving age) who are at or above each stage of development. For example, the *late concrete* line in Figure 2.1 shows that only 40 per cent of 10 year olds are at or above the stage of late concrete operational thinking, while nearly 90 per cent of children have reached this stage by the age of 15. In practical terms this means that in the last year of an average primary school, most material would have to be pitched at the early or mid-concrete level for some 60 per cent of the pupils. In the fourth form of an average comprehensive school, not more than 30 per cent of a genuinely mixed ability class are likely to have formal operational thinking available to them. The effect of 'creaming', the selection out of more able children by local grammar schools or independent schools, is to reduce the proportion of formal operational pupils in comprehensive schools even further.

· Now, genuinely mixed ability comprehensive school fourth forms are

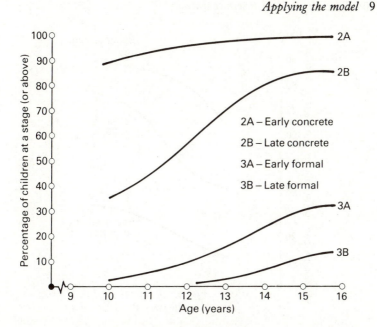

Figure 2.1 Proportion of children at different Piagetian stages in a representative British child population.

pretty rare things. From their third or fourth years a majority of schools practise some sort of streaming, banding, setting, or option choices which effectively separate pupils into groups of roughly similar ability. It will be difficult to predict the likely distribution of stages in such classes from the mean levels in Figure 2.1. What Figure 2.1 does not reveal is the enormous *variation* in the proportion of pupils at each stage found in different schools. If we consider only the attainment of early formal operational thinking, Figure 2.2 shows the percentage of pupils at or above this stage in three samples:

(a) the sample representative of all pupils in England and Wales (this is the same 3A line as on Figure 2.1)
(b) a sample drawn from grammar schools, selecting perhaps the top 15–20 per cent of the ability range; and
(c) a sample drawn from 'super selective', generally direct grant, schools which probably represents the top 8 per cent of the ability range.

The differences between these three populations is immediately apparent. Whereas the teacher of an average class of third formers cannot expect more

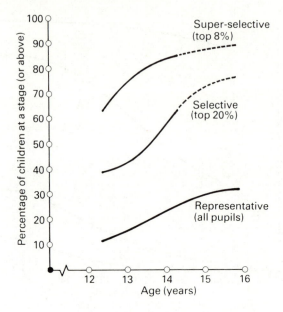

Fig. 2.2 Proportion of pupils showing early formal (3A) thinking in three different populations.

than 20 per cent of his/her pupils to have formal operational thinking available, the teacher in a selective school can rely on from 60 to 85 per cent of his class being capable of comprehending the sort of abstract models (particle theory, key-building processes) which characterise much of the Nuffield O level science curricula.

Since there are qualitative differences in the formal and concrete modes of thinking, the results summarised in Figure 2.2 seem to suggest that there should be a qualitative shift in the nature of the science taught as one goes from an 'average' class to a 'selective' one. It is necessary to pursue this suggestion further, especially when one remembers that by far the most popular science curriculum in use in all schools in England and Wales was derived directly from the Nuffield O level sciences, developed by trials in the most elite of grammer, direct grant, and 'public'[1] schools.

This leads us directly to a consideration of the analysis of science curricula for levels of demand. This is the necessary second half of the equation matching pupils to what is taught, and it has been the second major concern of CSMS.

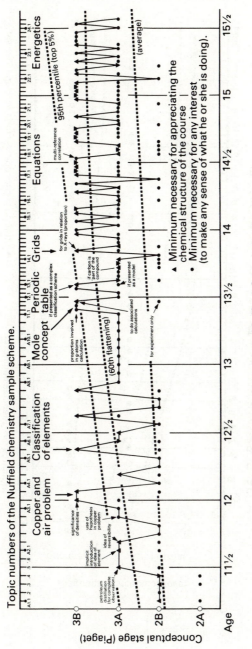

Fig. 2.3 Cognitive demands in Nuffield O level chemistry course.

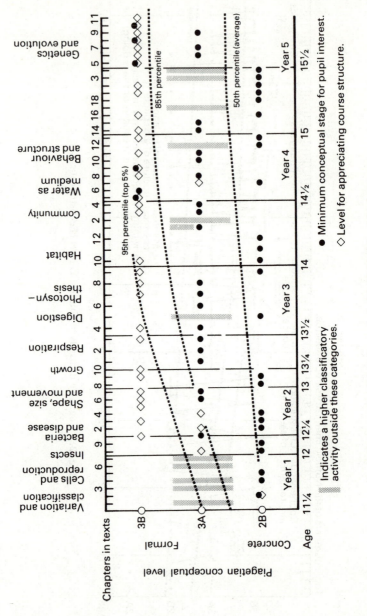

Fig. 2.4 Cognitive demands in Nuffield O level biology course.

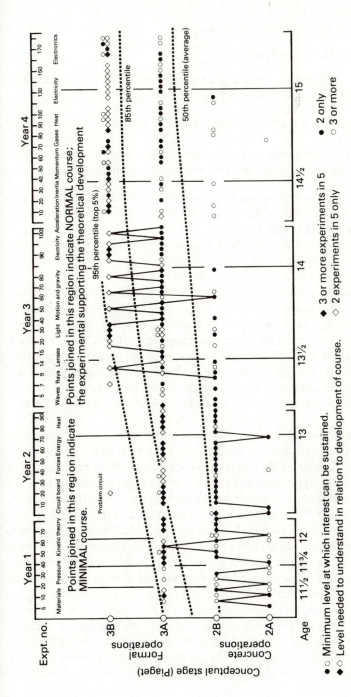

Fig. 2.5 Cognitive demands in Nuffield O level physics course.

Curriculum analysis

Between 1972 and 1975, one of us developed a system for assessing the level of thinking that a curriculum activity demanded:

(a) By use of a taxonomy derived from *The Growth of Logical Thinking* [21].
(b) By use of a taxonomy based on five categories of description such as, What relationships can children use?, Use of models, etc.

The scheme was applied to a number of well known science curricula, and the results published in the science education journals [20; 50]. Some are reproduced here (Figures 2.3–2.5).

More recently, CSMS has been developing the analysis method to make it readily available to all science teachers. This Curriculum Analysis Taxonomy (CAT) is described in full in Chapter 8.

The broken lines imposed on the curriculum analysis diagrams indicate the levels of thinking attained by (a) the average pupil, (b) the average selective school pupil (15 per cent of the whole population attaining level), and (c) the most able 5 per cent of the whole population. These lines are derived from Figures 2.1 and 2.2 above. On the curriculum analysis diagrams they show clearly that the games of the Nuffield O level science courses are generally out of reach of the average population throughout, and are even above the levels available in the selective school population for the first year.

Those teaching in selective schools might wonder at the message apparently contained in Figures 2.3–2.5. They might argue that the curriculum development of the sixties was a good example of the system adapting itself intelligently to change. By the end of the fifties the rate of change of science itself had outstripped both the teaching tradition of the universities and the O and A level syllabuses (in the major sciences the time taken for as many papers to be published as had been published before in the whole history of science had got down to between eight and twelve years). As each wave of newly trained teachers arrived in the schools, so the gap widened between the glimpse or experience they had had of fresh science, and the routines of school science.

So the impulse for change was from within the system, and in Britain the Science Masters Association and Association of Women Science Teachers (later amalgamated as the Association for Science Education, ASE) spoke for those teachers who wanted change. But it is worth remembering that these bodies represented almost exclusively the grammar, direct grant, and public schools. Their view of science in education dominated ideas of the purpose of science in schools for almost twenty years, throughout the whole traumatic period during which the British educational system 'went comprehensive'.

Within a surprisingly short time from the formation of subject committees by the SMA – AWST, proposals were formulated, and projects set up under the aegis of the Nuffield Foundation. Courses were designed, given trials in co-operative schools, new methods of examining were tested, and the final course materials handed over for publication. And yet it was not long before it was discovered that the Nuffield O level courses, for all their stimulating material, were not as well adapted to the whole range even of their designed target population as had been the traditional O level syllabuses and exams. It may be difficult to see how the empirical method by which they had been conceived and tested could have failed to produce courses well-matched to their teachers and pupils, but the reason is very obvious once it has been pointed out. It is simply a matter of sampling.

Ideally the trial schools should have been a random sample of schools from within the population of schools containing the target population of the new courses (the top 20 per cent). Then the problems which were revealed during the later revision commissioned by the Foundation would have been recognised at the time and dealt with. But in a selective school one gets accustomed to thinking of certain kinds of subject matters, or depths of treatment within a science, as natural to certain ages. One deals with the exceptions by calling the slower pupils 'dull', and promoting those who are very bright to a higher form. The model never becomes disconfirmed. Since the stages of science teaching are matched to the chronological and personality age of the pupils rather than to their present intellectual level, one tends to think of children as much the same everywhere, and that the cause of differences between the attainment of children from one school to another lies in the relative quality of the schools or the teaching in a department. Given this tacit model, the strategy of the Nuffield teams was correct. The sample of schools one would need would be those, of different types, which already had teachers predisposed to use the new materials in as profitable manner as possible; the purpose of the trials would be to locate inefficiencies in the process, not to check the match of course to pupil over a wide range of pupil levels.

It is not suggested that the Nuffield course writers were in any way culpable. The basic research on which much of this book is based was not published by Piaget until 1959, and it was not until 1965 that enough replications had been carried out and published to justify initiating any application research based upon it. Piaget's own account gave very little indication of the population distribution of the stages he describes with age; in fact you could read *The Growth of Logical Thinking* and decide that the Nuffield O level course designers had got it about right.

However, it is when we look at attempts to adapt the O level material for wide range groups in comprehensive schools that the most serious problems become apparent. We have all started with science—that is mostly school science routines—as we know it, and assumed that the strategy should be either to modify the tried and trusted methods we know, or to find out different ways of achieving the *same ends* (different, because the pupils cannot assimilate the 'academic' methods of teaching of the grammar school). But perhaps the truth is that, for the science course *content* we are used to (with the possible exception of much of traditional O level biology) the so-called 'academic' methods of teaching just happen to be the most efficient ways of teaching it.

Perhaps it is not just that the method of introducing the material must be changed, but that the nature of the science taught itself must be different. The difference between the most appropriate science courses for a sample of formal operational thinkers, and one for those who think in essentially concrete terms, is not just a matter of pacing, or of different numbers of steps to the same end. We believe that an entirely new curriculum model is required, from which different content and ways of handling it would follow.

NOTES

1 For non-British readers, we should explain that in the UK the term 'public' school means a private school.

Part 2

3 Concrete and formal operations

In Part 2 we will take a closer look at the characteristics of concrete and formal operational thinking (Chapter 3), and see in some detail how these characteristics are used to develop class tasks for assessing levels of thinking (Chapter 4). In Chapters 5–7 we will describe some of the uses that can be made (and have been made) of these class tasks.

Characteristics of the main stages of cognitive development

The important characteristics of, and differences between the main stages of cognitive development, which we have so far done little more than label, may be illustrated from Inhelder and Piaget's own reports of children's responses to a particular problem. Most of their investigations were based on activities which a child could undertake, comment on, and be questioned on. Thus it is not entirely coincidental that when they came to study thinking developments in adolescents, they frequently used topics and apparatus that are featured in secondary science courses. For example, most secondary science courses contain some work, usually practical, relating to the phenomenon of floating and sinking and to the concept of density.

This problem is introduced in Chapter 2 of *The Growth of Logical Thinking* [21] by giving each subject a variety of objects, such as pieces of wood, a needle, pebbles, a jar lid, some corks, and a candle, and for older subjects some blocks of the same volume but different masses and a plastic cubic box. The child is asked to classify the objects according to whether they will float or sink, to explain his basis for classification, and then to try them out in a bucket of water. Finally he is asked to provide a general explanation to account for the observation.

GIO (6 ; 0) "These things [previously classified] go to the bottom?" – *"Yes, that one"* [the wooden ball]. – "Why?" – *"Because it's heavy."* – "And these?" [the class of floating objects]. – *"That one swims because it's light."* We do the experiment with the cover. It floats *"because it's light."* – "And if you push it?" – [It sinks.] *"It's because it's light, and light things never stay on top."* – "And that plank?" – *"It will stay on top."* – "Why?" – *"Because it's heavy."* – "Why?" – *"Because it's big."* – "And if you lean on it?" – [He does.] *"It comes back up because it's light."* – "And this?" [large needle]. – *"It goes to the bottom because it's big."* – "And that [metal plate] if you push?" – *"It will stay at the bottom."* – "Why?" – *"Because it's light."*

[21]

This is an interview with a child who displays pre-operational thinking. In order to be in a position to solve the problem of why things float or sink, the child must first be able to classify successfully many objects into the class of floaters, or its complement, sinkers. Only then will it be possible to reflect upon the properties of those objects which will float. GIO knows perfectly well what he is doing with words which describe things. When he says that something is light one cannot doubt that it corresponds with his experience; it is not a noise made idly in the air. But there is a difference between saying that something is floating, and saying that *it belongs to the class of things which float*. The first is immediate, and just says what is, while the second involves something more than a descriptive act. It involves being able mentally to produce the class of floating objects, which in turn means being able to assign objects by their properties either to membership or to non-membership of that class. This is some kind of act: indeed, it is a mental act, since objects are not perceived bearing labels saying 'floaters' or 'sinkers'. Piaget calls such a construction upon reality an 'operation', and since GIO cannot use such an operation, he is described as pre-operational.

When GIO says that a lid 'floats because it is light', and then when it is pushed under and sinks says 'it's because it's light, and light things never stay on top' what he lacks is not accurate perception, but the implicit rules of classification which would not allow the same property to identify both membership of a class and non-membership of the same class. Further, these rules are unconscious; either a child has such a reality-processing mechanism or he does not, but in neither case is he self-conscious about it.

Here are some responses of a child who is beginning to use concrete operations:

RAB (7 ; 11) first classifies the bodies into three categories: those which float because they are light [wood, matches, paper, and the aluminium cover]; those which sink because they are heavy [large and small keys, pebbles of all sizes, ring clamps, needles and nails, metal cylinder, eraser]; and those which remain suspended at a midway point [fish]. "The needle?" – *"It goes down because it's iron."* – "And the key?" – *"It sinks too."* – "And the small things?" [nails, ring clamps]. – *"They are iron too."* – "And this little pebble?" – *"It's heavy because it's stone."* – "And the little nail?" – *"It's just a little heavy."* – "And the cover, why does it stay up?" – *"It has edges and sinks if it's filled with water."* – "Why?" – *Because it's iron."* [21]

The improvement of RAB over GIO is that, being in the early phase of concrete operations, he can classify consistently into the class of light things, and the class of floaters. Thus, Piaget says, he can correlate the results of two classifications. In the case of these two classes this means that he can become aware of these possibilities:

	Floaters	**Sinkers**
Light:	wood, matches, paper, aluminium lid, etc.	needle, pebbles, eraser
Heavy:	no examples given	keys, stones, clamps, metal cylinders

Yet the presence of the light sinkers prevents him from producing an explanation in terms of lightness.

BAR (9 years): [class 1] – Floating objects: ball, pieces of wood, corks, and an aluminium plate. [class 2] – Sinking objects: keys, metal weights, needles, stones, large block of wood, and a piece of wax. [class 3] – Objects which may either float or sink: covers. Later BAR sees a needle at the bottom of the water and says: *"Ah! They are too heavy for the water, so the water can't carry them."* – "And the tokens?" – *"I don't know; they are more likely to go under."* – "Why do these things float?" [class 1]. – *"Because they are quite light."* – "And the covers?" – *"They can go to the bottom because the water can come up over the top."* – "And why do these things sink?" [class 2]. – *"Because they are heavy."* – "The big block of wood?" – *"It will go under."* – "Why?" – *"There is too much water for it to stay up."* – "And the needles?" – *"They are lighter."* – "So?" – *"If the wood were the same size as the needle, it would be lighter."* – "Put the candle in the water. Why does it stay up" – *"I don't know."* – "And the cover?" – *"It's iron, that's not too heavy and there is enough water to carry it."* – "And now?" [it sinks]. – *"That's because the water got inside."* – "And put the wooden block in." – *"Ah! Because it's wood that is wide enough not to sink."* – "If it were a cube?" – *"I think it would go under."* – "And if you push it under?" – *"I think it would come back up."* – "And if you push this plate?" [aluminium]. – *"It would stay at the bottom."* – "Why?" – *"Because the water weighs on the plate."* – "Which is heavier, the plate or the wood?" – *"The piece of wood."* – "Then why does the plate stay at the bottom?" – *"Because it's a little lighter than the wood, when there is water on top there is less resistance and it can stay down. The wood has resistance and it comes back up."* – "And this little piece of wood?" – *"No, it will come back up because it is even lighter than the plate."* – "And if we begin again with this large piece of wood in the smallest bucket, will the same thing happen?" – *"No, it will come back up because the water isn't strong enough: there is not enough weight from the water."*   [21]

A child who is able to classify, such as BAR, can also do the same with lightness and bulk (or bigness).

	Small	**Big**
Light:		X
Heavy:	X	

He now has (as he had not before) the mental apparatus to reflect upon experience and, noting the presence of objects in the two cells marked by crosses, distinguish between the absolute weight of objects and their inherent heaviness (the small, heavy objects). This is what lies behind the emergence of the familiar conservations, in this case of weight and its associated concept, the global density or 'heaviness' of materials. It seems to take a couple of years for the developing concrete thinker to realise these concepts from his own experience. BAR uses very flexibly the strategies that appear at the consolidated, or late concrete operational stage. The typically mechanistic explanations appear, the problem is set up in terms of opposing forces, and so on. The reason for this, Piaget says, is that the other construction upon reality which is an aspect of concrete operations is seriation—the ability to order objects according to their length, their weight, their brightness, etc. Once this becomes habitual the child can solve two-variable problems such as that involved in Hooke's law. By noting the 1:1 correspondence between the heavier weights and the spring, he can 'explain' the relation as 'the heavier the weight, the greater the stretch'. In this case BAR is able to construe the problem in terms of opposing forces, that of the object with a push down, and that of the water opposing it.

One should note that operations such as classification and seriation are not primarily acts of language, although words are used as their tools. Most adults have learned to use such operations so instantaneously and habitually that they have forgotten the time when they did not, and that they have transformed reality for themselves in learning to use them. These operations are described as 'concrete' operations, since they operate only on the immediate properties of things.

So, is concrete operational thinking, with its ability to classify and order a series, sufficient to produce a full solution to the floating/sinking problem? BAR can clearly use concrete operations, and yet one can see his mind twisting and turning and yet unable to produce a consistent description that explains the results. His last remarks show that his explanations will not yield access to the solution and are, indeed, false predictions as well.

The problem is that the variables which need to be considered are not directly observable. The very immediacy of the explanations produced by BAR are a hindrance to his seeing the real issue. He needs to be checked by a more subtle sense of contradiction than he possesses. When he puts the large block of wood in the water and finds that it floats, this does not worry him as it should. Instead he invents the ad hoc explanation that it is 'wide enough not to sink'.

FRAN and ALA show a further advance in their approach to this problem:

> FRAN (12 ; 1) does not manage to discover the law, but neither does he accept any of the earlier hypotheses. He classifies correctly the objects presented but hesitates before the aluminum wire. "Why are you hesitating?" – *"Because of the lightness, but no, that has no effect."* – "Why?" – *"The lightness has no effect. It depends on the sort of matter: for example, the wood can be heavy and it floats"* And for the cover: *"I thought of the surface."* – "The surface plays a role?" – *"Maybe, the surface that touches the water, but that doesn't mean anything."* Thus he discards all of his hypotheses without finding a solution.
>
> ALA (11 ; 19): "Why do you say that this key will sink?" – *"Because it is heavier than the water."* – "This little key is heavier than that water?" [the bucket is pointed out]. – *"I mean the same capacity of water would be less heavy than the key."* – "What do you mean'" – *"You would put them* [metal or water] *in containers which contain the same amount and weigh them."* [21]

In contrast to BAR, FRAN tests the hypothesis that it is lightness which makes objects float by saying 'wood can be heavy, and yet it floats'. Earlier the difference between RAB and GIO could be marked by the latter not having the rules of classification which show him the contradiction of using lightness to characterise both floaters and sinkers. Now the difference between BAR and FRAN is that the latter knows that to test the possibility that all light things float, it is not so important to produce examples of light things floating as it is to look for an example which might disprove the hypothesis.

Piaget explains this in terms of what he calls *formal operations*, a further mental construction not so much directly on reality itself, but which allows reality to be critically examined from a sense of the many *possibilities* that it contains. Not only might there be light floaters, light sinkers, heavy floaters, and heavy sinkers, but from the combination of them that exists one can estimate the degree of relatedness between any of the properties. In this case a formal operation enables FRAN to know that if both light floaters and heavy floaters exist, there is no necessary connection between lightness and floating. As with classification and concrete operational thinking, it is not suggested that the process is conscious.

And yet lightness and heaviness must have something to do with it, and one can see BAR, the concrete thinker, trapped by trying to compare the weight of the object with the weight of water in the container. He lacks the contradiction test shown here by ALA which is to note that if things float or sink whether there is a large or small bucket the quantity of water must be irrelevant. Before the weight of the object can be compared with the weight of its own volume of water the child must have formed a concept of the volume of an object as distinct from its particular shape. This entails another aspect of formal operational thinking: the ability to handle the more complex problems with three (or more) variables, where at least two can be varied independently.

An elementary example of this is concepts that are ratios of two variables, in this case density. Whether the solution to the floating problem comes from comparing the weight of an object with the weight of the same volume of water, or whether it comes from comparing the weight/volume ratios of objects and water, weight and volume have to be clearly distinguished and then related. We have confirmed many times over that children who are just late concrete (2B) predict that of two rectangular blocks, one made of brass and the other the same dimensions made of clay, the brass one will displace more water because it is heavier.

To get the beginnings of a solution the child must first scan through the various objects, with their weights compared to their volumes, so as to see why small, light, but dense objects sink. Taken through the set of objects as a whole the volume and weight are partially correlated but independent variables in relation to the set. Then he must relate these to the weight of the volume of water equal to the volume of each object. ALA (early formal) is nearly there, and one could certainly say that he and FRAN can use the density concept. They could, for instance, appreciate the apparatus and experimental structure provided by the Nuffield Combined Science Course, given assistance in organising the collection of data. We have confirmed this, and report the details in Part 3.

LAMB (13 ; 3) correctly classifies the objects that sink: *"I sort of felt that they are all heavier than the water. I compared for the same weight, not for the same volume of water."* – "Can you give a proof?" – *"Yes, I take these two bottles, I weigh them. . . . Oh!* [he notices the cubes] *I weigh this plastic cube with water inside and I compare this volume of water to the wooden cube. You always have to compare a volume to the same volume of water."* – "And with this wooden ball?" – *"By calculation."* – "But otherwise?" – *"Oh, yes, you set the water level* [in the bucket]; *you put the ball in and let out enough water to maintain the original level."* – "Then what do you compare?" – *"The weight of the water let out and the weight of the ball."*   [21]

But it is only LAMB, who is operating at the late formal stage (3B), who produces a general solution and only such children can spontaneously convert it into a measurement explanation using the apparatus provided. Thus it is likely that only late formal operational thinkers can make use of the opportunity to use newtonmeters in an investigation to achieve an understanding that means something to them. Confirmation of this also is described in Part 3.

This development of the ability to think through the floating/sinking problem is exactly what many teachers have found for themselves, empirically, with second and third year pupils. Piaget provides an explanatory framework for such findings, and we will show later how the findings and the framework may be formalised and used in curriculum reform and the development of teaching strategies.

Three tiers

In looking critically at as detailed and complex a body of research as that which originates in Geneva, it is useful to distinguish three levels at which the reports are made, levels of increasing abstraction from the data. Both the value of the Piagetian model for our present purpose, and our ability to defend it against much telling criticism, depends on an appreciation of these three *tiers*.

Piaget and his co-workers over a period of fifty years observed many hundreds of children in close detail, watching their performance and monitoring their responses, sometimes in natural settings but more often in task situations such as the floating problem illustrated above. At the first tier, then, there is the actual description of pupils' responses themselves. Just to read through some of the interview protocols is itself an enlightening experience for any teacher or parent.

At the second tier, Piaget fits these observations into a stage-developmental pattern. A child's responses to a task are seen as arising from the set of cognitive structures which he has available, and the structures which cause early concrete responses to one task will be responsible for responses to another task which can also be characterised as early concrete. To this tier also belong the postulates about the mechanism by which cognitive structures develop and change with age and experiences.

The third tier we describe as the *metatheory*. A metatheory is a higher level theory which explains or accounts for lower level, more concrete theories. In this sense the Bohr atom provides an adequate metatheory for the Mendeleev periodic table, and natural selection is a metatheory which helps to account for evolution. The periodic table and evolution are themselves theoretical models, but they are a level closer to the raw data than are the Bohr atom or natural selection. Piaget's metatheory is expressed in symbolic logic and it is at this level, for instance, that he accounts for the features of formal operations in terms of the logical operations of Implication, Negation, Reciprocity, and Compensation—the INRC group.

The temptation to devise an economical metatheory is enormous. The periodic table, evolution, and stage theory are messy, complicated things which are difficult to grasp and cumbersome to use. It is the nature of scientific investigation to search for simpler, more embracing models from which we can predict the features of the intermediate models, and so the behaviour of reality. However, although Piaget's attempt at a metatheory looks frustratingly near a solution, almost everyone who has looked deeply into this problem believes that actual human thinking is much richer and more varied than any logical calculus can model.

Because of this uncertainty associated with the tier 3 metatheory, we have based all of our empirical work on the tier 1 accounts of tasks and interviews, and on the tier 2 general description of stages based directly on them. Since it forms the foundation of much of our work, we should take a closer look at the tier 2 general accounts of concrete and formal operational thinking, especially with respect to two areas of concern to science teachers: the handling of multi-variate problems, and the construction of hypothetical models.

VARIABLES

Concrete thinkers tend to treat all associations as 'equivalence relations': if B happens with A, then A will happen with B. The rules of equivalence relations are the same as those of simple causal relations where only two variables are concerned, but as soon as a third variable is involved, then A may *not* happen with B; C may do instead. The formal thinker somehow knows that the fact that two aspects are associated has not necessarily defined their relationship, and that further investigation is required before a decision can be made. In the case of a pendulum, if you change both the weight and the length, then it may not have been the change in weight that caused the period of oscillation to change. If the pressure in a gas is raised then the volume will drop. But does a drop in volume mean that the pressure has gone up? Not if there is a third variable involved, such as temperature.

Concrete operational thinking involves putting considerable structure on reality, and most of us conduct our everyday business using concrete thinking only. Where its rules are adequate to the situation it is successful. The problem comes when its rules are not adequate. In the pendulum problem the relation between the length and period of oscillation is discovered because this happens to be an equivalence relation. But the fact that the pendulum weight and angle of swing are *not* significant variables is not discovered because it is the nature of concrete thinking to find only the kinds of relation that concrete thinking can process. Thus it is being suggested that one important difference between concrete and formal thinking is the qualitative change in complexity in moving from one independent variable to situations where two or more are involved.

It could also be said that each level of abstraction added in effect creates an extra variable to be dealt with. In a balance beam the relation between the mass hanging on one end of the beam to the mass hanging on the other end is direct; the relation between the distance from the pivot point of one mass and of the other is also direct. However, multivariate thinking is involved in answering the further question about the relation between these two relations.

The development of formal operational thinking could be seen as the change that is required in going from bivariate reality to tri- or multi-variate reality. (Pre-operational thinking could be seen as the ability to cope only with univariate reality, with some associations and close neighbours providing temporary linkages.)

MODELS

The use of models can be illustrated with a study of the development of heat concepts in 10-13 year olds which we carried out. Here we had both ample empirical data, and evidence of the Piagetian levels of the children studied. Two clear conclusions emerged: the concept of a temperature scale was completely formed by the late concrete stage, while the use of a 'caloric' model, the establishment of a concept of an amount of heat which could be transferred from one body to another, did not emerge until the early formal level. Why is the first concrete and the second formal?

The distinction seems to be that between causal thinking and thinking requiring a model. In causal thinking there is no gap between the two aspects of reality related. Whether it be the extension of a spring by different weights or the moving up of a thermometer thread by hotter objects, the relationship involving only one independent variable *is* the explanation. 'The heavier the longer; twice as heavy, twice the extension' and 'the hotter the higher; how high up the thread goes measures how hot the object is'. Such formulations look for no further explanation and could be described as 'concrete modelling'. The characteristic of concrete thinking is that the classifications or orderings imposed on reality only involve two aspects or variables at a time, and one of them is treated implicitly as dependent.

As soon as there are three or more variables to be considered, of which one can arbitrarily be regarded as dependent, the number of possible relations becomes such that some kind of model is required around which to conceptualise the relationship between them. In order to handle heat and temperature relationships on the mixing of two bodies the masses and temperature changes of both must be used together. Producing some kind of heat fluid model in terms of which what is lost by one is gained by the other seems to be connected with the process of distinguishing the mass and the temperature as two independent variables. Concrete modelling involves imposing a structure (either numerical or classificatory) on reality itself; formal modelling is comparing reality with an independent set of rules and assumptions and looking for their correspondences. At the concrete stage the concept of temperature has to do double duty as both the intensive (potential) and extensive (quantity) properties of heat, and so no adequate model is formed. One can probably generalise the process of conceptualising any energy change in terms of intensive and extensive factors as requiring formal thinking.

An important point to note about the nature of cognitive development as described by Piaget is that the successes of each stage are incorporated in the next stage. Thus the strategies of each successive stage include those strategies of the preceding stage which have been found to be useful in modelling reality.

More detailed accounts of the characteristics of each stage and sub stage of cognitive development are given in Chapters 8 and 9, together with many specific examples of the types of science learning activities that are

available at each stage. For now, these general accounts of the nature of
formal and concrete operational thinking are adequate as an introduction to
the methods developed for estimating the thinking levels of groups of
pupils.

4 Class tasks

It is being proposed that there is a serious mismatch between science curricula and pupils' abilities, but before you can believe in this you must believe in the description of the school population displayed in Figure 2.1 (p. 9). Such data concerning the levels of cognitive development in a representative sample of the whole school population has never been available before. It is fair to ask why this should be so, given the maturity of Piaget's theory of cognitive development, but as soon as one considers the traditional method of assessing a child's level of thinking, by an interview lasting from fifteen to forty minutes, it becomes obvious that it is an impossibly laborious and expensive method for assessing an adequately large sample. The only practicable way of assessing the thinking processes of 12 000 pupils is to develop tasks that can be given to a whole class at a time.

Development

Now, in any attempt to transpose the clinical method into a class task one must take note of the essential features of the Piagetian interview. These include:

- the use of apparatus that provides feedback to the child following his/her suggestions and predictions;
- the ability to question the subject on the reasoning underlying his/her responses;
- observation of the child's reaction to counter-arguments or proposals of alternative explanations;
- some allowance for flexibility in questioning following the child's responses.

In the development of a class task which purports to achieve similar ends to the clinical interview, one would do well to try to preserve as many of these features as possible. In addition, an ideal class task should be able to assess pupils on a five or six point scale from early concrete to late formal operational thinking, including intermediate levels such as 2A/B (mid-concrete) and 2B/3A (transitional to formal). What is more, it should yield this assessment directly from a consideration of the item responses, since it is the quality of a response which makes it characteristic of one stage or another. However many 2B responses a subject may give, they cannot eventually add up to a 3A total.

CSMS were not the first to try to develop group tasks to test cognitive development. However, when we inspected others' attempts, we found that they either failed on a number of the criteria described above, or else there were serious practical difficulties in their administration. For instance, paper and pencil tests of the logical processes associated with concrete and formal operations we rejected both because of our doubts about the validity of Piaget's metatheory and because they failed to provide the subjects with the essential feedback from apparatus in action. At the other extreme, tests in which each child has his own set of apparatus have obvious practical difficulties, and also leave open the question of the accuracy with which the child will record his actions and observations. Such considerations led us to the development of *demonstrated* class tasks, which have come to be known as **Science Reasoning Tasks**—SRTs. [35]

Administration

Giving an SRT would be a familiar experience to most science teachers since it is far more like teaching a well structured demonstration lesson than it is like administering a test. Indeed, one of our aims in their development was that the tasks should be available to teachers who have no special training in Piagetian psychology or in the administration of interviews.

The administrator has a set of apparatus large enough for all to see clearly. He performs experiments with the apparatus and asks certain questions as he proceeds. The precise wording of the questions is not critical and they can be modified or reworded within certain limits to ensure that all have understood what is being asked. (This has an extra advantage in situations where English is not the first language of the subjects. Here the question can be given verbally in the vernacular without the problems that are entailed in translating precisely worded objective test items.) Each pupil has a response sheet on which the administration questions are summarised and which has space for a constructed response, or a list of possible answers from which to choose one. Constructed responses may require simple drawings or short sentences.

Most items are based on questions originally described by Inhelder and Piaget, and almost every one is designed as a specific indicator of the attainment of one stage or sub-stage of cognitive development. Thus a '2B question' is one which is likely to be answered correctly only by subjects who are capable of late concrete operational thinking. Tasks vary in the range of stages that they assess. One SRT (Task I) contains a mixture of 1B, 2A, and 2B items; another (Task II) is made up of 2A, 2B, 2B/3A, and 3A items, and the remainder (Tasks III to VII) contain items in the range 2B to 3B. Tasks may be selected to suit the age and ability of the class being assessed.

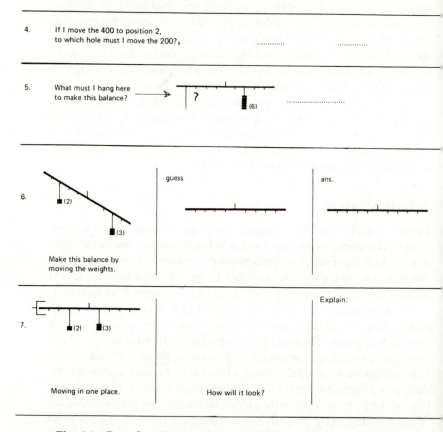

Fig. 4.1   Part of pupil's answer sheet for SRT4 equilibrium and the balance.

Scoring rules are quite simple in that almost every item may be marked either right or wrong, and the administrator's guide specifies clearly what is to be considered as a correct answer. The assessment of a pupil is based on the number of items she has correct at each stage. Assessment rules are spelled out in detail in each task guide, but in general a two-thirds pass criterion is used, so that four out of six 2B items are accepted as indicating the attainment of late concrete operational thinking. A pupil with four out of six 2B items, and two out of four 3A items might be described as 2B/3A, transitional to formal, since he has not quite reached the necessary criterion for a 3A assessment.

An illustration

As an illustration, consider the Equilibrium in the Balance task (SRT IV). In Chapter 11 of *The Growth of Logical Thinking*, Inhelder and Piaget describe a simple beam balance apparatus in which weights can be hung from holes at various distances from a central pivot point. The subject is set a series of practical problems concerned with making the beam balance with different weights at different distances from the pivot. At the same time she is asked to make predictions about what would happen under different conditions, to explain what does happen, and to formulate general rules relating weights and distances at equilibrium.

In the SRT developed from this task the administrator has a simple demonstration beam balance made of a metre rule pivoted at the centre, with holes drilled to take weights at intervals either side of the pivot. There are 13 scored items in this task, and a typical series of these items would be as follows (the relevant part of the pupils' answer sheet is shown in Figure 4.1).

4. Pupils are shown that the beam balances with this arrangement:

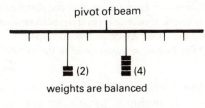

weights are balanced

Fig. 4.2

The 400 g weight[1] is moved out to hole 2, and pupils are asked where the 200 g weight must now be placed to make the beam balance again. They record their answer by drawing in the '1st try' box of no. 4.

Now the administrator moves the 200 g weight out one hole, saying something like 'I moved the 400 g weight out one hole, so maybe it will balance if I move the other weight out the same amount'. When it is seen that this does not work, pupils are allowed a second try at the answer.

5. This item is done without using the apparatus. The administrator talks through the question on the pupils' sheet, explaining it as necessary, and the pupils draw their answer.

6. This arrangement is set up:

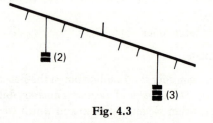

Fig. 4.3

Pupils are asked to 'guess' where the weights must be positioned to make the beam balance. When they have done this, they are shown the correct solution and told to record it on their sheets.

7. The balanced solution to no. 6 is now clamped, and then each weight is moved in one hole. Taking care to make sure that all have seen exactly what was done, pupils are now asked what the balance will look like if the clamp was removed. When they have all done this by making a drawing in the left hand box on their sheet, the clamp is removed. This is a nice moment, usually greeted with some surprise and some rejoicing. Pupils are now asked to explain *why* the balance goes down on the 200g side.

What sort of cognitive processes are required to answer these items correctly?

The example just described (unequal weights and distances) is resolved at sub-stage 2B not yet by metric proportions (with the occasional exception of the relationship between 1 and 2) but by *qualitative* correspondences bordering on the equilibrium law: 'The heavier it is, the closer to the middle'.

[21, p. 171, our italics].

Here and elsewhere Piaget shows that the concrete thinker can quantify the weight/distance relationship at equilibrium only when a simple 'two times' strategy can be applied. It is just this strategy that is required for items 4 and 5, and so these are considered to be 2B items.

Items 6 and 7 cannot be solved until the subject has effectively discovered the law $w_1d_1 = w_2d_2$, since the ratio of the weights is not just 'two times'.

Inhelder and Piaget show that this is possible only at the early formal stage, and quote one subject who expresses his discovery like this:

You put the heaviest weight in the position that stands for the lightest weight. [21]

In other words, a 3-weight must go in hole 2 to balance a 2-weight in hole 3. Unlike items 4 and 5, the solutions to items 6 and 7 demand that the pupil sees equilibrium as a function of two fully independent variables, and so 6 and 7 in this task are 3A items. The 3B items take the problem further and seek an explanation in terms of work: the weights multiplied by the vertical distances that they travel. 3B items also test the pupil's ability to formulate and quantify the ratio concepts involved in reaching equilibrium, and in work.

Altogether, SRT IV has three items at 2B, seven at 3A, and three at 3B. A subject who gets two 3B items right is considered to be late formal; four or more at 3A or 3B indicate at least early formal thinking.

There are some features worth noting from this illustration: firstly, that pupils have an opportunity to learn during the task. In question 4, after one 'free' try at the answer, they are shown one very plausible answer which is *not* correct. In items 6 and 7 they are shown correct answers after they have made their attempts. If they have the mental structures necessary to discover the law, they have plenty of opportunity to do so during the course of the task, whether or not they have met the problem before. This raises the question of the influence of previous learning:

'We might say that it is a matter of book learning but, in contradiction, we are able to present some examples...in which the proportionality schema is organized before any academic knowledge enters.'   [21, p. 172/3]

In the CSMS work we not only confirmed that finding on a much larger scale, but also the converse: even pupils who had formally 'done' the law of levers were not able to achieve a 3A or 3B rating in the task unless they were actually able to use metric proportions in a new situation. In the pendulum task (SRT III), a knowledge of the formula $2\pi\sqrt{\frac{L}{g}}$ alone *cannot* lead to success on any item. The structure of the tasks does not allow a pupil who has learned the algorithm, and can get the correct answer to conventional physics problems on the topic to succeed on the formal items unless he can really use formal operations.

Testing the tasks

From the examples shown here, it might seem that we followed the lead of

Table 4.1 CSMS Science Reasoning Tasks: Summary of Characteristics

No. and Name	Content	Range	No. of items	Internal consistency[1]	Test-Retest corr.[2] (n)	Task-interview corr.[2] (n)
I Spatial Relationships	A drawing task. Child's perception of verticals, horizontals, and perspective.	1–2B+	4[3]	.82	—[4]	.85 (7)
II Volume and Heaviness	Conservation of substance, weight, and volume. Proportionality as density.	1–3A	15	.78 (.83)[6]	(.84)[6]	—[4]
III The Pendulum	Control of variables; deduction of effects of weight, length, push on time of swing.	2B–3B	12	.83 (.84)[6]	.79 (24) (.76)[6]	.71 (24)
IV Equilibrium in the Balance	Inverse proportions in the balance problem. The work principle.	2B–3B	13	.84	.78 (31)	.55 (18)
V The Inclined Plane	Inverse proportions in the truck-on-slope problem The work principle.	2B–3B	14	.76	.82 (32)	.63 (15)
VI Chemical Combinations	Combinatorial thinking, deductions from evidence.	2B–3B	16[5]	.76	.64 (28)	.65 (23)
VII Flexible Rods	Control of variables; deduction of effects of length, thickness, shape, material, weight on bending of rods.	2B–3B	17	.86	.85 (38)	.79 (23)

NOTES

1. KR20 internal consistency for all except Task I, for which Hoyt's analysis of variance used. Ns. = 380 for I, 240 for II, and 560 for remainder.
2. Correlation adjusted to correspond to range of internal consistency sample.
3. Each scorable at several levels.
4. Not assessed.
5. One item scorable at three levels included as 3 items.
6. Figures obtained by Johnson (1977) using 67 grade 10 students in Saskatchewan.

Piaget somewhat uncritically. This is not the case, and in this section we will outline some of the ways in which various aspects of the validity of the SRTs was established.

During the evaluation process we were able not only to confirm in a large measure the accuracy and consistency of Piaget's description of characteristic responses at different stages of thinking, but also to identify some instances where the Inhelder/Piaget account is not supported by evidence. There are cases where we find pupils able to use concrete strategies to solve problems which they believed to be formal, and others where a response they describe as being stage-related turns out not to be correlated with cognitive development. For example, in the chapter on chemical combinations, Inhelder and Piaget suggest that from five bottles of liquids, the number of combinations selected for testing by a subject is an indication of their stage of thinking. In fact this proved to be true in only a very loose sense, and we found that the initial combination chosen by the subject was not closely correlated with the stage of cognitive development as determined by other measures.

This example illustrates an important distinction between the clinical interview and the group task. The former allows a very probing investigation of the child's thinking processes, and it is certain that the stage developmental model of cognition could not have been developed without it. On the other hand, the class task, by increasing the numbers of subjects whose responses can be sampled, allows the statistical methods of psychological measurement (psychometrics) to be applied to the model. Some aspects of this will be touched on in the remainder of this chapter, but for more technical accounts the reader is referred to the original papers [51; 57].

DISCRIMINATION

A good SRT item should be a sharp discriminator. This means that ideally a stage N item should be passed by all subjects who are at stage N or above, and failed by all those who are below stage N. If the percentage of subjects at each stage who get an item correct is shown on a diagram, then Figure 4.3 represents a good discriminator (in this case at 3A), while Figure 4.4 is a rather poor discriminator for our purpose. It is true that more pupils at higher stages get it right, but the trend is general and not specific to the onset of a particular way of thinking. In the development of an SRT, items which behaved like that in Figure 4.4 would be modified or discarded.

Percentage of
pupiis at
each level
succeeding
on item
100
80
60
40
20
2A
2B
2B/3A
3A
3B
Piagetian level of pupils

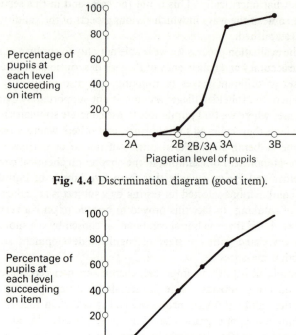

Fig. 4.4 Discrimination diagram (good item).

Percentage of
pupils at
each level
succeeding
on item
100
80
60
40
20
2A
2B
2B/3A
3A
3B
Piagetian level of pupils

Fig. 4.5 Discrimination diagram (poor item).

RELIABILITY

Two aspects of this were checked as each SRT was developed. The internal consistency, as measured by the Kuder-Richardson coefficient r_{tt}, was used as a check that all of the items in a task were telling the same story. Perfect internal consistency is indicated by an r_{tt} value of 1, and SRTs have r_{tt} values in the range 0.7 to 0.8 (see Table 4.1). As the number of items in a task are reduced one would expect the internal consistency coefficient value to fall. If, when a particular item is omitted from the calculation, r_{tt} rises, it shows that the item omitted is behaving inconsistently—being passed by people who fail other items, and failed by people who pass others. Such an item, which might also have an item discrimination diagram (above) with a negative slope, would be discarded or radically modified.

Test-retest reliability is used as a measure of the extent to which a task will tell the same story on two successive occasions. The same group of pupils were given the same task twice with a three to six week interval between administrations. For each task the correlation between the relative grades ascribed by the task to the pupils on the two occasions was satisfactory, and this is important evidence of their reliability.

VALIDITY

The crucial question about SRTs is whether or not they measure what they purport to measure. That is, are they valid instruments for assessing the stage of cognitive development of pupils?

The tasks certainly have face validity,[2] in that they are developed directly from Piagetian protocols. SRTs contain items corresponding to all of the described behaviours in the chosen Piagetian task. Over a period of forty to fifty minutes the subjects are taken through the task so that every aspect is shown to them. They probably get more systematic feedback than they would typically give themselves if they were conducting the investigation in front of an interviewer. In this way each of the SRTs is essentially 'the same' as the original Inhelder and Piaget task.

That SRTs do measure much the same thing as do the clinical interviews was shown by a study of task-interview correlations. A sample of the pupils who had taken each task were interviewed individually, following Piagetian protocols. Correlations between levels ascribed by the tasks and by the interviews are included in Table 4.1. Not only are these quite satisfactory, but further analysis of the data indicates that the mean stage given by task is not significantly different from that given by inteview, and that the group tasks are actually more reliable than the interviews as a method of determining stage of cognitive development. We believe that this arises because of the extra source of variance provided by the personal interaction in the interview.

Further evidence for the validity of SRTs is given by task-task correlations. If one or more of the tasks was measuring significantly a factor unrelated to cognitive development, then correlation between the tasks would be low. This is not the case. On the whole a child who was rated as formal operational on the balance beam problem was rated the same on the other problems also: when five tasks were given to a sample of 500 pupils it was found that the agreement between them was most satisfactory. Since this point has important implications for stage theory in general, we will devote a separate chapter (7) to it, and details of the correlation are given there.

The final test of the validity of the Science Reasoning Tasks is provided by their ability to predict the success or failure of individual pupils with bits of the science curriculum that have been analysed to determine the level of demand that they make. This test of predictive ability will form the subject of Chapter 6.

NOTES

1 We found generally that the pupils tested were not sufficiently familiar with the correct units of weight (newtons) for this rather loose terminology to bother them. We are of course referring to the weight of a 400g mass but felt that to make this proper distinction would have added an extraneous source of confusion.
2 *Face validity* is the validity which arises from the appearance of the test. Since the apparatus and questions are closely similar to those described for the clinical interview, it is, on the face of it, reasonable to suppose that the tests could measure the same thing as the interviews.

5 Using Science Reasoning Tasks

Nationally

The availability of valid and reliable class tasks for assessing Piagetian levels has opened the way for large scale surveys of school populations. Between 1974 and 1976 such a survey was conducted of the 9 to 16 year-old population of England and Wales. The tasks used in this survey were:

Task I *Spatial Relationships.* A drawing task which investigates pupils' perception of verticals, horizontals, and perspective. It is suitable for younger children, in the range from pre-operational to late concrete operational thinking.

Task II *Volume and Heaviness.* This task incorporates many of the best-known Piagetian conservation tasks, including how the amount of substance in a clay bell, its weight, and its volume as measured by displacement are seen to vary as its shape and position vary. Density concepts are investigated also. This task covers the range from late pre-operational to early formal operations.

Task III *The Pendulum.* This is a classic science activity, used to investigate the child's ability to control variables and to deduce the effects of weight, length, and amplitude on the period of swing, from a series of matched demonstrations. This is the first of the SRTs that covers fully the formal operational period, and it can be used to assess pupils in the range from mid-concrete to late formal operational thinking.

In the national survey, Tasks I and II were used with younger pupils (approximately 9-11 years) and Tasks II and III with the older ones. Two tasks were given to each pupil, to increase the reliability of assessment. The survey included classes from 24 comprehensive schools drawn from the Cardiff area, Gloucestershire, Hertfordshire, Lincolnshire, Manchester, Staffordshire, Nottinghamshire, and Southampton. These were from both rural and urban environments, although none were large metropolitan comprehensives of the type found in Inner London. Thirteen middle schools from the Leeds area were included, and also nine selective (grammar, direct grant, and 'public') schools.

Every class in at least one year of each school was tested. Not every child did both tasks because of absences, but a good idea of the total number of children tested can be gained from Table 5.1 which shows the total number in each age group whose Task II results were used in the analysis.

Table 5.1

Group	Mean age (years)	No. taking Task II	
A	11.0	765	(831 took Task I)
B	11.1	1157	
1	12.1	1727	
2	13.1	2094	
3	14.1	1238	
4	15.3	487	(642 took Task III)
5	15.9	346	(548 took Task III)
		Total 7814	

All of the tasks were administered by the science teachers in the schools, after a briefing by a CSMS team member.

We have claimed that the results shown in Chapter 2 are for a 'representative' population. We should explain the basis for this claim. In each of the schools used in the survey, the *Calvert Non Verbal Reasoning Test* was given to all of the 11 year-old group in the school. The Calvert test had been standardised by the National Foundation for Educational Research (NFER) to have a mean of 100 and a standard deviation of 15 on a population truly representative of 11+ pupils in England and Wales. Thus the mean Calvert score for each school would give an indication of how that school's intake rated by national standards. If our sample had turned out to have a mean Calvert score of 100 and standard deviation of 15, we could have rested content that it was indeed representative. Since it turned out in practice to have a slightly higher Calvert mean than this, it was proposed initially to discard from the sample one or two schools with high Calvert means, until the total sample mean was 100. However, this seemed wasteful of hard-won data, and so, since Calvert means were closely correlated with the percentages of pupils at 2B, at 3A, and so on, we were able to plot regression lines of cognitive development on Calvert scores, and read off an estimate of what would be the proportion of pupils at each stage for a population with a Calvert mean of 100. For example, for group 3, the schools' Calvert means and percentages of pupils at or above the stage of late concrete operational thinking were plotted as in Figure 5.1. The percentage of pupils at or above 2B and 3A can then be read off for the representative population that has a Calvert mean of 100.

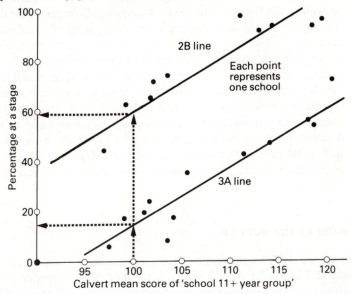

Fig. 5.1 Example of regression lines for determining % at a stage in population with a Calvert mean of 100.

It can be seen that the Calvert test was used as a primary standard, and our representative results obtained from it as a secondary standard. Chemists will see the analogy of this to the method of standardising a hydrochloric acid solution by titrating it against a sodium carbonate solution that has been made up to be standard from the weighed, dry, solid.

WHY SRTs?

At this point a reader may ask why, if an intelligence test correlates well with measures of cognitive development, was it necessary to develop SRTs at all? Would the well-known IQ tests not have done the same job more simply? They would not, for two main reasons:

1 Intelligence tests are age-related. They do not give an absolute measure of mental development, but one which compares a child's mental functioning to that of all other children of the same age. SRTs are not age-corrected, and give an absolute measure of stage of cognitive development.

2 More importantly, an IQ test says very little about the *quality* of thinking of the subject. A score of 120, say, says little more than that the subject is in the top 9 per cent of the ability range. On this information alone it will not be possible to predict the way that the subject is likely to tackle problems in science. Any measure of cognitive development, whether class tasks or interviews, is based on analysis of the child's thinking strategies and may be used, as we have shown, as a reliable indicator of the sort of problem that the subject will be able to solve. An intelligence test is a statistical device based on the discovered, but not explained, correlation between the ability to do well in IQ tests and scholastic achievement. Measures of cognitive development provide comprehensive information on the *quality* of thinking.

Results of the survey

What can we say about the results of the survey, which are summarised in Chapter 2. Figures 2.1 and 2.2 on pp. 9, 10 show how the proportion of children at each stage of cognitive development changes with age, both for the population representative of national norms, and for populations in selective schools. Three features of these results are worth comment at this point: the age at which each stage is attained by the 'average' pupil; the apparent levelling off of cognitive growth in the last year or two of compulsory schooling; and the range of levels found at any age.

AGES AND STAGES

The first feature that will strike anyone accustomed to the conventional college accounts of Piagetian theory is that the average ages at which each stage is attained is far higher than that usually quoted. Most potted Piagets will tell you that 'concrete operations are attained around the age of 9, and formal operations about the age of 12 to 14'. The results show clearly that by 9 years only about 30 per cent of pupils are using concrete operations fully, and one must go to 14 years before this rises above 75 per cent. At 14 years only 20 per cent are using even early formal operations.

The common misconceptions about the ages of attainment of each stage arise, naturally enough, from Inhelder and Piaget's own accounts of interviews with children, where the ages are quoted in years and months as if they were highly significant. The Genevans say very little about their sampling, and in fact it is not of great importance. Piaget has described in detail the characteristics of each stage of cognitive development, giving responses typical of each, and so has established a comprehensive theory which describes and accounts for the development of cognitive functioning. The techniques they developed were unique in their power for probing thinking processes, but were not appropriate for the establishment of population norms. SRTs, developed on the backs of the Genevans' experience, by allowing groups to be tested have made possible another level of application of Piagetian theory.

So, we claim that we have established norms for the population of England and Wales, and that the ages of attainment of each stage are significantly higher than those suggested by Piaget.

DOES COGNITIVE GROWTH STOP AT 15?

The second notable feature of the results is the levelling off at 14 or 15 of the proportion of pupils who can make use of formal operations [53]. A simple extrapolation would suggest that in the adult population only 30 per cent ever make use of theoretical models, or can handle multivariate problems, or can use any of the cognitive strategies characteristic of formal operational thinking. This would be contrary to the Piagetian implication that everyone attains the stage of formal operations eventually.

How well justified would such an extrapolation be? We simply cannot answer this question without more evidence. The majority of children in England and Wales leave school soon after their sixteenth birthday, and those who stay on are, in general, the more able pupils who are aiming for higher education. Thus it becomes technically difficult to obtain a sample for testing which is representative of, say, all 18 year-olds in the population. Any scenario proposed for cognitive development patterns in the post 16 year-old population would be speculative, and so out of place in this section —but see Chapter 12 (pp. 137).

THE RANGE OF ABILITIES

To some extent, this third feature of the results mediates the effects of the other two. Within any age group, because of the great range of Piagetian stages that will be found, it is easy to identify a significant minority whose development with age conforms closely to the classical Piagetian model. This minority used to be found in the grammar schools, when children were selected to go to one type of school or another according to their performance in aptitude tests at 11 +. The necessary corollary to this finding is that, amongst the comprehensive school population, there is a significant minority who are much further behind the stages traditionally given for each age than is shown even by the norms of the representative population.

Piaget concedes that some children show formal operational behaviours very early, but he treats the problem of population distribution of stages as of minor importance. Presumably, he made the same assumptions as it is natural for a selective school teacher to make about the matching of intellectual development with general psychological and physiological development. This was questioned early on in Lovell's replication study of *The Growth of Logical Thinking* [32], but it was not until the CSMS survey that evidence was available to show how different from anticipated was the spread of Piagetian levels in the growing child population. As in Lovell's study the accuracy of Piaget's descriptions was confirmed, but the ages at which different children attained each stage conforms to a quite different model.

Some children (2%) show early formal thinking behaviour as early as 10; yet even by the age of 14 the incidence of this level in the child population is less than 25%. For late formal thinking the figures are even smaller: 1.5% by 12.3, and 7.1% by 14.4. If the children are arranged in percentiles, with those attaining the later Piagetian stages at the earliest ages at the top, what emerges is an astonishing differential in development among the child population, and an absence of any necessary association of formal operational thinking with adolescence.

If we take the attainment of early formal thinking by the middle of the Third Year as the criterion that a pupil is able to participate in a traditional O level course timed in the school in the traditional way (since this is the point by which the basic concepts of the science will be introduced), the lowest percentile which fits the requirement is the 80th (that is, the top 20%). One seems to have met that figure before. The 95th percentile (top 5%) is something like 3 years ahead of the 80th percentile, in terms of age of attainment of the higher Piagetian stage, and the 80th percentile is about 3 years ahead of the 50th percentile (the strictly average pupil) who, in turn, is about 3 years ahead of the 20th percentile (the bottom 20%). Thus Piaget's picture of human development must be modified very considerably. The top 10% of the population has a development from concrete to formal operational thinking which antedates their physical adolescence; the population between the 90th and the 80th develops more or less as Piaget describes. The 70th percentile are unlikely to develop beyond early formal thinking by the end of adolescence, and below the 60th percentile (the top 40%) it is unlikely that they will develop beyond concrete operational thinking during the compulsory school period, although the developmental curves do show a marked acceleration with the onset of physical adolescence. Yet the developmental *sequence* Piaget described is confirmed, as it has been by all studies which have had the aim of testing it.

It is now possible to see how the problem of sampling, introduced in Chapter 2, was there most acutely even for the development of the O level courses designed for the top 20% of the ability range. If the 95th percentile (the top quarter of the selective school population) is three years ahead of the 80th percentile, it would be very easy, working empirically in terms of what one knew one's pupils could manage, to produce a course two or three years out of phase with the development of the course's target population. And if one asks the question, where would the SMA and Nuffield Foundation find the best teachers that were available, it is not unreasonable to answer that they are teaching a very biased sample of the target population! If the graphs for the conceptual demand level for the Nuffield O level chemistry course are examined, and compared with the population growth curves, it will be seen that the course writers have achieved an excellent match with the 95th percentile.

But this is to get ahead of ourselves. The demands made by curricula are discussed in more detail in Part 3, and in Chapter 11, Part 4.

Locally

The last decade has seen a growth of local education authority or even individual school curriculum development programmes. It is being recognised that while the centralised national curricula can provide teachers with valuable resource material, the enormous diversity of environments, of school facilities, and of pupils' interests and aptitudes makes it difficult to adopt such national curricula wholesale. Now, the great range of levels of development found within each age group makes it a risky business to use the national results presented here to predict the likely levels you will find in a particular class or a particular school or group of schools.

Early in the process of setting up the parameters within which a new science curriculum is to be set, Science Reasoning Tasks can be used by the teacher in the target schools to obtain a profile of stages of development which the curriculum should suit. As we mentioned in Chapter 4 on the development of SRTs, they are designed to be given by science teachers, and no special understanding of Piagetian psychology is required. Thus a survey of a section of the school population that is to be the target for curriculum reform is well within the capability of any school or local authority.

SRTs have already been used in Britain and in many other parts of the world (notably the West Indies, the Philippines, Swaziland, South Africa, Nigeria, West Bank-Palestine, Kuwait)[1] for local surveys. The purposes of such surveys include the provision of information for curriculum developers; investigations into causes of difficulties with existing science curricula; and research into possible relationships between aspects of culture and language on the one hand, and cognitive development on the other. More details of the way that SRTs have been used in what could have been the formative evaluation on one science curriculum in Britain are given in the next chapter.

NOTE

1   For fuller references to many of these overseas uses of SRTs, the reader is referred to Adey, P.S. *Science Curriculum and Cognitive Development in the Caribbean* PhD University of London, 1979.

6 Selecting attainable objectives

We have shown (Chapter 4) how group tasks were developed from Inhelder and Piaget's accounts of childrens' performances on science-like tasks. And we have presented (Chapter 2) the results of a national survey of the school population made in 1976/77 using these tasks. Of what use is this information to the teacher, especially to the teacher of science? How can a knowledge of the cognitive profile of a class, a school year, a locality, or the country help teachers to improve the quality of their offerings?

Two of the many possible answers to these questions are:

(1) that it helps teachers to *select*, from all of the curriculum material that is available, material that is most appropriate for their particular pupils, and
(2) for teachers and others who are developing their own curricula, it helps in the selection of objectives and the construction of activities which are realistic and stimulating.

In this chapter we will illustrate how these two answers can be worked out in practice, with accounts of two investigations carried out in English schools.

Predicting achievement

In illustrating the first answer above, we will also be presenting evidence for the predictive validity of the tasks themselves. If the task says that none of *this* group of boys seems to use formal operations, and if they are shown consistently to fail to achieve the objectives of a curriculum activity which demands formal operations, then possibly the task is telling the truth. The example which follows shows how the tasks may be used to predict the failure or success of pupils with some of Nuffield Combined Science.

Three sections of the course were investigated:

Section 4: **Air**
Section 6: **Water**
Section 8: **Earth**

For each section, a sample of pupils was chosen and given one or two Science Reasoning Tasks, so that an estimate could be made of their stages of cognitive development. They were then taught the unit, the teachers being asked to follow as closely as possible both the letter and the spirit of the curriculum as it is presented in the printed guide.

The Nuffield Combined Science Curriculum does not have lists of behavioural objectives spelled out for each activity of each unit. Nevertheless, from the general description of what is expected to be achieved by each activity, and by the simple expedient of asking 'What is the point of doing *that*?', one can specify the implied objectives quite closely. For example, the objectives of the first few activities of Section 6 could be summarised as follows:

1a Use newtonmeters to determine the apparent loss in weight of objects when lowered into water.
 b Use the results of 1a to arrive at some rule (theory) for determining whether an object will float.
 2 From various chemical reactions involving water and steam, arrive at a model of water as a hydrogen-oxygen compound.
3a Discuss the design of experiments to find out how plants use water.
 b Find out where the water loss in plants takes place.
 c Estimate the water through-put per day of a tree.

DEMAND LEVEL

Now, if one reads these objectives in the light of the Inhelder/Piaget accounts of children's responses to tasks, and of the general characteristics of formal and concrete operational thinking that Piaget derives from such responses, one can ascribe a demand level to each objective. Here we are using the tier 1 and tier 2 (p. 25) accounts of cognitive development to determine the type of thinking that is required to achieve each objective.

What follows naturally from such a categorisation of objectives is that a pupil who has not reached the necessary stage of cognitive development cannot attain that objective. This is a prediction, and one that is eminently testable, in the sense that it can be falsified. It gives us an opportunity to lay on the line both our claims to be able to assess pupils' levels of cognitive development, and our claim to be able to assess the demand levels of curricula. Are the predictions borne out?

The study of NCS Section 6 will be used to illustrate the method of testing this prediction. The distribution of pupils who followed NCS Section 6 was found, by SRTs II and III, to be as follows:

Number at **2A**	(early concrete) :	4
2A/B	(mid-concrete) :	18
2B	(late concrete) :	30
2B/3A	(transitional) :	24
3A	(early formal) :	10
	Total :	86

Initially, a total of 52 items were written to test the objectives of the unit. As each objective has a cognitive demand level associated with it, so does each corresponding test item. Of the original 52 items, 11 had to be discarded either because they were much too difficult or much too easy for all of the pupils, or because they failed to discriminate effectively between pupils who, overall, did well on the test and those who did badly. Note that this 'test development' was performed in the light of results from the test itself, and without reference to the estimated stages of the pupils.

The 41 items left in the test covered objectives with demand levels as follows:

2A: 7
2B: 8
3A: 13
3B: 13

A global measure of the success of the prediction made by the SRT on the likely performance of pupils is given by the correlation coefficient between pupils' levels as given by the SRT and their performance on each level of item in the NCS6 examination. The value obtained was $r = 0.78$, indicating the high predictive power of the SRTs.

More detail of the results can be provided by looking at the percentage pass rate of pupils at each level, as estimated by SRTs, on items at each level as assessed by curriculum analysis. This is shown in Table 6.1.

This table shows, for instance, that the mean pass rate of pupils at or below the middle stage of concrete operational thinking ($\leq$ 2A/B) is 39 per

Table 6.1   Nuffield Combined Science Section 6: Percentage pass rate of pupils at each level on items at each level.

Pupils at	No.	Items at: No. of items:	2A 7	2B 8	3A 13	3B 13
2A	4 ⎫					
2A/B	18 ⎭		39	15	3	0
2B	30		51	34	11	2
2B/3A	24		67	56	24	7
3A	10		87	80	47	10

cent on items testing objectives which make early concrete demands. But the same pupils achieve a pass rate of only 15 per cent on items demanding late concrete (2B) thinking. The thick line running across the table from upper left to lower right divides the cells in which high success rates are possible (lower left) from those in which the theory predicts that high success rates are unlikely. Clearly the predictions are substantially borne out, and the estimates of pupil stage made by the SRTs are good indicators of success on curriculum objectives whose demand levels have been analysed. One should note that a demand level being within a pupil's reach is not in itself a guarantee of success. It is simply an indication that, given the right learning experiences, attitudes, and physical facilities, he/she could reach that objective. It is thus easy to explain percentages less than 100 in the lower left section of the table. The 24 per cent success rate of 2B/3A pupils on 3A items is understandable, since 2B/3A is transitional to the formal stage. None of the remaining success rates in the upper right hand section could be considered high enough to falsify the predictions made, given the accuracy of the estimates made by the SRTs and the assessment of curriculum objectives.

Teachers of mixed-ability classes will appreciate a further significance which emerges from these figures. Table 6.2 shows the facility (percentage pass rate) of pupils at 3A, and of pupils at 2B, on the items which test objectives assessed as demanding 3A. Note that these pupils are from the second year of a comprehensive school with a somewhat above average intake, and that all have had the same teaching. Their different rates of success are therefore most likely to be attributable to their difference in cognitive levels.

Table 6.2 Facility of 3A items testing Combined Science Section 6 for two groups of pupils taken from one class.

Pupil level	Item numbers											
	1b	*1d*	*1f*	*1h*	*1i*	*2h*	*3e*	*3f*	*3h*	*5d*	*6i*	*6j*
Stage 3A (N = 8)	63	38	63	63	25	0	83	75	13	25	38	63
Stage 2B (N = 10)	0	0	20	20	0	10	20	20	10	0	0	30

Allowing for the usual imperfections of existence, most teachers would probably feel that the sample of activities which the items represent were well-chosen for the 3A pupils, and almost completely unsuitable for the 2B pupils.

Similar results were obtained for NCS Sections 4 and 8. An extra problem that arose with Section 8 will be discussed in Chapter 11, but the reader interested in details of the Section 4 and 8 work is referred to an article in *Studies in Science Education* [54] where the research aspects are studied in more depth, and to another in the *School Science Review* [55] where some fine detail is given of childrens' performance in biology, chemistry, and physics objectives from the three sections.

Attainment of course objectives

Both in the study reported above, and in a later study reported in Chapter 10, the attainment of specific course objectives was related to the Piagetian level of the pupils. In Figure 6.1 discrimination diagrams are shown (see Chapter 4, p. 38, and Chapter 10, p. 112) for items relating to objectives 1, 2, and 3 summarised on p. 50. In this way the level of cognitive demand of the objectives can be checked. In the diagrams the pupils are first grouped by their Piagetian level on the SRTs used. For each group of pupils the percentage who passed items relating to the objective is plotted. The level at which the success-rate becomes appreciable is a measure of the cognitive level demanded by the objective. From 6.1a and 6.1b it can be seen that objective 1b makes a late formal (3B) level of demand. For objective 2, that of arriving at some kind of predictive 'hydrogen-oxygen' model of water, items relating to some aspects of the objective demand 3A competence, and others 3B (6.1c). Objective 3a is shown in Figure 6.1d. Here item 3b refers to a question which asks for design of an experiment with a suitable control to allow for the water which might have evaporated anyway from the jar in

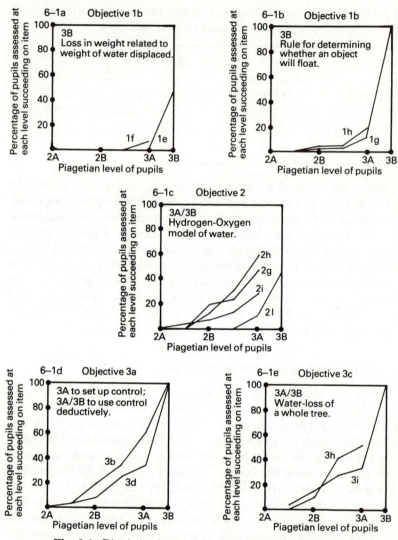

Fig. 6.1 Discrimination-level diagrams for NCS6 objectives.

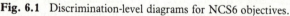

which a leafy branch was placed. This is well within the capacity of those pupils with 3A competence. But to make valid quantitative deductions from such experiments (item 3d) is nearer a 3B level of demand, and the same applies to objective 3c (Figure 6.1e).

The significance of the high level of thinking required for the attainment of these characteristic objectives from Section 6 of the Combined Science course will be discussed later in Chapter 11. The point to be emphasised here is that an approach which began as a test of the predictive validity of SRTs has considerable power as an interpretation of the results of trials of new or experimental course material. This is now developed further.

Formative evaluation

In the previous section the performance of children who had been taught a well-known science course was interpreted in terms of their cognitive levels as assessed by SRTs. In this section a general method is outlined by which initial trials of experimental course activities can be evaluated in terms of cognitive-level-matching of objectives to pupils.

A group of teachers in Leeds [31] is working towards the production of teaching objectives in science for each year of their middle schools (age range 9 to 13 years). As a first step they have prepared, through a long process of discussion, detailed sets of objectives in twenty-one topic areas which they thought might be desirable for children to have attained by the time they leave the middle school. The next step in their work would be to find out empirically whether all of their objectives are attainable, and in which school year it is most desirable to introduce different aspects of the objectives.

CSMS took this as an opportunity both to develop a general method of formative evaluation which might be used more speedily to interpret the results of any teaching trials carried out in the schools, and also to carry out empirical studies on the attainment of concepts in areas of science which had hitherto not been the subject of formative research.

The process may be illustrated with the topic of *heat*. Firstly, a study of the Leeds objectives, and of a conceptual inventory described by Erikson [12], enabled nine categories of objectives to be identified:

(a) composition of heat
(b) conduction effects
(c) expansion effects
(d) matter/heat differentiation
(e) understanding of the temperature scale
(f) change of temperature
(g) temperature/heat differentiation
(h) change of state
(i) knowledge of particular temperatures

For each category, sets of test items were written of varying difficulty. From pre-trials of the total heat test thus devised, with 9 and 12-year olds, items could be ranked according to facility—high facility items being the ones that most children could pass. By looking at the facility of the items within each of the nine categories, it became possible to distinguish three levels at which each category could be understood. For instance, for area (a), the levels might be described as in Table 6.3.

Table 6.3 Description of levels of understanding of Composition of Heat, and items used to generate description.

Level	Description	Items used
I	Heat is understood in terms of what it is associated with, e.g. melting, heating, expansion	8b 7d 9b
II	Heat can be equalised on mixing. However, it is still confused with amount of substance	3a 7f 8c
III	Heat is differentiated from amount of substance, and temperature, and can be handled in simple calorimetric calculations	10b

Having identified the existence of these levels in some categories, further items were written to explore the whole range within each category, and some modification was made to existing items to clarify their meaning. Following trials of this test, further adjustments were made to improve the discriminating power of each item *within its category*. This was done by classifying pupils as essentially level O, I, II, or III on their performance on the total set of items within each category, and then determining the extent to which each item accurately discriminated between pupils at one level and those at the next. Item discrimination diagrams similar to those described in Chapter 4 and Figure 6.1 were used.

This process gave a test of 65 items, in nine categories. Within each category the level at which the item discriminated was known. This test was administered to about one hundred and ninety 9 and 12-year olds. Analysis of the results showed that across all categories of heat objectives, there is only one significant factor. A more technical account of this study is given elsewhere [58], but the important point to note here is that a pupil who copes with the higher level accounts of heat phenomena in one category (say, conductivity effects) is most likely to cope with higher level aspects in other areas also. The importance of this result is that it argues for the existence of one determining factor in the comprehension of ideas in heat. Since it is most unlikely that all pupils will have had the same levels of learning experiences in all areas, previous teaching is unlikely to be the determining factor.

What does control the level at which different pupils are able to internalise concepts within the topic of heat? By now, it will not surprise the reader to learn that, in addition to the heat test, the pupils in this experiment completed an SRT—Task II, Volume and Heaviness. The SRT gave an estimate of their Piagetian level of development, and it proved possible to map stage of development on to the level of understanding of heat. Correlation between the heat test and Piagetian level was high ($r = 0.74$). Not only is the heat test unifactor within itself, but also with Piagetian development. The developmental sequence appears to be invariant, regardless of the previous experience or learning of the child.

It is only a small step further to look at pupils' achievement on the SRT, and on the heat test, and so correlate the levels of understanding of heat with Piagetian stages of development. Level I in each category corresponds roughly to early concrete, 2A; level II to late concrete; and level III to early formal operational thinking.

DESCRIPTIONS OF LEVELS OF DEVELOPMENT

From the descriptions given under the separate categories global descriptions can now be made at early and late concrete and early formal levels of development (Table 6.4).

There are three points here which are worth emphasising. Firstly, the process of development of the heat test does not necessarily lead to a unifactor test. The discrimination of items was sharpened within each category, not over the test as a whole, and had it been the case that different pupils with different previous experiences developed one aspect rather than another, factor analysis of the heat test would have revealed at least one factor for each sizable group of subjects' experiences.

Secondly, this approach to the description of the attainment of concepts by children does have the advantage that its results can be generalised from the group studied to other children. Because the results are classified according to developmental levels, prediction of attainment of these concepts by children of other ages and abilities can be made simply from

Table 6.4 Understanding of heat concepts at different Piagetian levels.

Early to Middle Concrete

For Heat, understanding is phenomenological. It is associated with burning, melting, etc. Expansion of gases may be seen in terms of hot air rising, and because expansion of solids is seen phenomenologically, it is not associated with the necessity of reversibility on cooling. Conduction may be different with different materials, and with mixing situations the hot gets cooler, and the cool gets warmer.

For temperature, on the other hand, the 1:1 mapping of temperature onto a linear scale is seen qualitatively, and is soon seen semi-quantitatively—'the higher the hotter'. Some, but not all, grasp temperature as an intensive property, e.g. on mixing a liquid at 25° with another at 25° the resultant mixture will be at 25°. But some add the temperatures.

Late Concrete

At this stage temperature is well-conceptualised and quantitative, with multiplicative relations between temperature changes and changes in length of thermometric liquid. Heat is associated causally not only with the obvious effects (more heat has more effect) but also with less obvious ones such as conduction in gases. Expansion is now understood as a reversible phenomenon. Fuels can be recognised, and it can be realised that oxygen (or air) is necessary for their combustion, and that some fuels are not renewable.

Yet since heat is conceptualised causally, a model of it is not developed at this stage. Thus Heat, Amount of Substance, and Temperature tend to get collapsed under the single concept of Temperature. Provided only one independent variable is involved the process will be correctly conceptualised. e.g. The more the amount of liquid/solid, the more heat will be required to heat it up, and the more heat that is put into a given object, the hotter it will get. Although the *intensive* aspect of Temperature is well-conceptualised, the *extensive* aspect of Heat is not.

Early Formal

Interest in *how* Heat causes its effects leads to the construction of models for conduction, expansion, heat transfer, etc. A more or less explicit model of heat flowing as a liquid from body to body allows quantity of Heat, Mass, and Temperature to be differentiated, with two being used as independent variables in simple calorimetric calculations, i.e. quantity of heat is a multiplicative function of both mass and temperature. Thus Heat now becomes an *extensive* property. The production of heat in chemical reactions is seen as an irreversible process, and the distinction between an endothermic and an exothermic process can be made, e.g. heating a fuel to ignite it, and then receiving heat from its combustion. At this stage theory can be used in contradiction of immediate experience: although the steel blade of a spade left outside overnight 'feels' colder than the wooden handle, it is recognised that their temperature must be the same, and that the difference in feel is due to the greater conductivity of the steel.

Table 6.4 (cont.)

Yet not more than one in five of the twenty-three 11 to 13 year-olds who produced concepts at the above level offered kinetic theory models of conduction, heat transfer, or gas expansion, and only one in two thought of expansion of solids in terms of greater movement of particles. Conduction was usually treated in terms of a 'heat-fluid', caloric model.

---

information on the developmental level of the latter. The advantage of this approach is that a descriptive and a normative account of the hierarchies involved is given simultaneously which is very rarely the case in the research literature. But there is an important problem incurred by this procedure, which is related to the third point.

Unlike the subject matter of the Piagetian group-tests (SRTs) which is related to a child's experience only in a very general kind of way, heat is a topic where the developmental descriptions of levels of understanding which we publish are likely to be attained fully only by those children who have had some specific experiences (probably in school lessons) on which their minds can impose structure. If a child is estimated at the 2B level by an SRT it will not necessarily be the case that he would succeed on all or most of the 2B items in the heat test. In effect we are describing the probable limit to a child's competence, given his level of development. In the data-interpretation some allowance had to be made for the performance of something like 30 per cent of the children lagging behind what one might have predicted for them from their performance on the SRT, Volume and Heaviness. But this does mean that one can specify, with a high degree of confidence, the lesson activities which would be most likely, for each level of child, to make him or her reach their present potential. This point will be taken up further in Part 4 of this book when the implications of the research are discussed.

In the last phase of the CSMS research this method of formative evaluation has been applied to the topics of *Structure and Forces*, and *Ourselves* from Science 5-13[46], since many teachers had asked for help in selecting linked sets of activities from the Science 5-13 source materials which would be most likely to be both stimulating and comprehensible to their middle school pupils. At the time of preparation of the manuscript of this book this was still 'work-in-progress'.

7 The unity of formal operations

We cannot conclude this section on the use and validity of Science Reasoning Tasks without facing a fundamental question about the Piagetian model of cognitive development, upon which all of our work rests: How general is development from one stage to the next?

The metatheory

This is the point where Piagetian theory becomes very controversial, and it would be worth taking a small diversion to spell out the different levels at which arguments about this have ranged, before presenting our own evidence and conclusions. Piaget describes ten 'schemas' as underlying the performance of subjects on the different types of experimental problems which provide the research base for *The Growth of Logical Thinking*. These schemas and the problems in which they are used are given below:

Control of variables:
  Investigation of many-variable problems—pendulum, flexibility of rods, many biological and social science problems.
Exclusion of irrelevant variables
Combinatorial thinking
Notions of probability
Notions of correlation
Coordination of frames of reference
Multiplicative compensation (moving one weight further from balance point counteracted by more weight on other side)

Equilibrium of physical systems
Proportional thinking
Physical conservations involving 'models' (e.g. displacement volume)

Clearly the first two group together, as do the middle three, and the last five. Moreover the first five are all involved in various ways in the biological and social sciences.

For Piaget, the preliminary description of 'schemas' was made only as a step towards showing the unity of the underlying structure of thinking responsible for all of them, named formal operational thinking. As Piaget's work developed the emphasis came to be less on cognitive levels of subjects, and more on the underlying structure of the thinking by which the subject relates to the outside world—indeed 'constructs' it. The search for this structure proceeds by an analysis of the logic involved in these ten schemas, and it leads to the metatheory which we described in Chapter 3 as the tier 3 level of generalisation.

Critics of Piaget find in the failure of the metatheory to produce falsifiable predictions grounds for rejecting the whole body of descriptive psychology produced by the Genevans. Some American science educators (notably Robert Karplus and Anton Lawson) go further, and take the view that there is *no* underlying unity of the ten schemas and they therefore prefer to describe them as the various 'reasoning patterns' by which different aspects of scientific thinking are performed. As our own approach has many similarities to theirs it is worth spelling out in some detail how it differs and, in so doing, provide an answer to the critics.

The controversy may be seen as a boundary dispute between the methods of traditional sciences including biology, and the social sciences which date from the end of the last century. Since our own ground and that of Piaget was exactly on the intersection of the two, it would be expected to attract the fire of both. The bulk of Piaget's experimental work has been done in the tradition of descriptive biology, whereas his theoretical model has been drawn from mathematics, as is usual in physics. Some psychologists, from what might be called the 'softer' end of the social science spectrum, have criticised Piaget for producing what appears to them a positivist account of human thinking. They claim that it fails to give a picture which allows for human invention and creativity, and that it appears unduly rigid in the predictions that it makes. Such critics include the Marxists. Since Piaget was very sensitive to this line of criticism, his own writings in the last twenty years showed a steady retreat from an earlier position which did imply a considerable degree of predictivity of human behaviour.

On the other hand, psychologists from both the behaviourist and the psychometric traditions have produced the opposite line of criticism— namely that Piaget's account of the development of thinking is not predic- tive enough. Viewed from the standpoint of the traditional sciences, they wish to make their subject approach the rigour of physics, which is more than the development of the discipline justifies. It did take three hundred years for physics to develop the power that it now has. It would be very nice if Piaget's metatheory had the general predictive power of atomic physics and chemistry. It would be the first psychological theory which did. In general behaviourist psychology achieved predictive power only at the expense of extremely narrow empirical generalisations. Something more modest seems in order. If, in a hundred years, psychology can produce something of the power of the periodic table in chemistry, it has done very well. This is the view we take of Piaget's life-work.

At the same time, we find it impossible not to agree with the 'hard' psychologists that the essential test of Piaget's theories must be quantita- tive. Thus we respect the very nice quantitative study [30] in which Lawson and Karplus have shown that the logical model, when expressed in testable terms, does *not* predict students' behaviour on tests expressing the schemas or reasoning patterns referred to above. But the essential unity of formal operational thinking does not depend only on the logical model. Our accept- ance or rejection of the idea of generality of cognitive development need not be based on the grounds of whether Piaget's metatheory explains beha- viour. Rather, the quantitative test which should be employed is that of *consistency between schemas*, and the predictive power from tests utilising two or more of the schemas to tests of understanding of science. In other words, we argue that the most useful test of Piagetian theory for science teachers is one at the 'tier 2' level. If that can be validated then we have a theory whose internal consistency can usefully inform practice.

If the reasoning patterns were each separate skills then it would not be expected that pupils with facility in one would necessarily have facility in another. Moreover, whether a pupil had ability in, say, physics, would depend on whether he possessed skill in specific patterns such as propor- tionality and the control of variables. Thus the degree of correlation *between* the schemas would be expected to be *low* on this view, while correlation between specific schemas and different sciences would be *high*. Proportion- ality should have little predictive power for biology. On the alternative Piagetian model the schemas merely express describably different aspects of an underlying multivariate thinking capacity, called formal operational thinking. Thus pupils with a high competence in one schema would be expected to have high competence in all the others. Moreover the schemas should all have relatively high and non-specific predictive power for understanding each of the sciences of physics, chemistry, and biology. Thus the Karplus-Lawson view makes a different quantitative prediction from the interpretation of Piaget just sketched, and the difference is testable. Moreover, the quantitative test just described is equally applicable to the objections of the psychometrist critics. If formal operational thinking is a unitary psychological construct, a factor analytical study of several tests embodying the schemas would produce one factor only, whereas if the critics and Karplus and Lawson are right, then each schema should produce a separate factor, expressing the relatively low correlation between the factors. Such quantitative tests have been carried out.

By 1978 CSMS had developed a total of seven Science Reasoning Tasks, five of which were based directly on experiments described in *The Growth of Logical Thinking*. Each of these tasks covered the range from before late concrete operations (2B) to late formal operations (3B), and each incorporated elements of more than one of the eight schemas described above. It thus became possible, by giving all five tasks to the same sample of pupils, to check whether their performance on different tasks, and across tasks on different schemas, correlated well with one another.

The sample used consisted of about 370 boys and 180 girls (counting only those who completed all five tasks). These were chosen from the third forms of comprehensive and grammar schools, and one independent school. The sample was selected from the more able since the national survey (Chapter 2) indicated that this group would be likely to contain a full spread of pupils in the 2B-3B range. The design of this experiment is deceptively simple, and it must be remembered that it could not have been carried out before a range of good group tests of formal operational thinking had been developed. Furthermore, anyone who has engaged in such a survey will recognise the formidable logistical problem of giving five tests, each taking forty to sixty minutes, to pupils in six different schools, in the London area, Dorset, and Bedfordshire. All of the tasks were administered by members of the CSMS team (P. Adey, M. Shayer, H. Wylam), but the enthusiastic cooperation of the science teachers and the pupils in the schools was an essential condition for the success of the testing programme.

The results of this exercise may be shown in two ways. Firstly, how well do the five tasks agree with one another in their categorisation of pupils into stages of cognitive development? Table 7.1 shows the percentage of the sample at each level given by each of the tasks:

64   *Towards a science of science teaching*

Table 7.1 Percentage of sample (N = 550) at different levels on tasks.

Task	2B⁻	2B Late concrete	2B/3A	3A	3B Late formal	Mean* level
Pendulum	4.3	18.4	28.0	27.6	21.8	3.44
Equilibrium in the balance	4.9	18.9	21.8	36.6	17.8	3.44
Inclined plane	7.8	20.3	20.7	38.5	12.7	3.28
Chemical combinations	5.4	15.2	27.7	38.8	12.8	3.38
Flexible rods	6.7	14.3	22.4	38.5	18.1	3.47

* based on coding 2B⁻ = 1 up to 3B = 5

Although the agreement is good, this gives only a global picture of agreement about numbers of pupils at each level. To see if the different tasks assign the same individuals to the same levels, results were subjected to factor analysis. On the model used, the total variance is partitioned between the common factor variance (communality) and the variance unique to each task. An estimate of the error variance was available from test-retest data so it was possible to estimate the proportion of specific variance for each task to the common factor variance. This is shown in Table 7.2, which seems to justify the use of a unifying construct such as operational thinking to describe what these five tasks have in common.

Table 7.2 Estimates of specific and common variance for five tasks.

Task	Communality	Test-retest R	Specific variance
Pendulum	0.52	0.78	0.26
Equilibrium in the balance	0.56	0.77	0.21
Inclined plane	0.61	0.81	0.20
Chemical combinations	0.53	0.65	0.12
Flexible rods	0.74	0.85	0.11

The second way in which the supposed unitary nature of formal operations can be investigated is to look within each task for the items which test the different schemas. Factor analysis of eleven such within-task item clusters again shows one outstanding factor which accounts for 39.2% of the total variance. Factor loadings for the 1st and 2nd factors, and communality, are shown in Table 7.3.

Table 7.3 Factor analysis of 11 within-task clusters (unrotated).

Task	Variable	Factor 1	2	Commun-ality
Pendulum	Control of variables	0.64	−0.24	0.47
	Deduction of effects	0.63	−0.22	0.45
Equilibrium in the balance	Proportionality	0.70	0.22	0.54
	Equilibrium of system	0.63	0.28	0.47
Inclined plane	Proportionality	0.65	0.22	0.44
	Equilibrium of system	0.62	0.16	0.42
	Work interpretation	0.49	0.29	0.32
Chemical combinations	Combinations	0.31	−0.11	0.11
	Strategy and deduction	0.67	−0.14	0.47
Flexible rods	Control of variables	0.74	−0.21	0.59
	Compensation	0.68	−0.11	0.48

The only one of these item groups which does not hang together well with the others is the ability to think of possible combinations of four liquids, part of the task on Chemical Combinations. Piaget suggests that this ability is a characteristic of the child's stage of thinking but results here, supported by experience during the development of this task, indicates that this is not so. The ability to think of all possible combinations of four liquids (or coloured beads, or of four independent conditions for growing seedlings) is not closely related to stage of cognitive development. This is an example of the way that psychometric methods can be used to enlarge on, develop, or make minor corrections to the original accounts of cognitive development given by Piaget and Inhelder. Not all of the behaviours that they observed and reported upon turn out to be stage-related, and their specification of behaviours at each stage is not invariably confirmed.

But the main conclusion to be drawn from the results shown in Tables 7.1–7.3 is that formal operations *does* hold together as a unitary construct.

The critics have been shown to be wrong by their own psychometric methods. Formal operational thinking is a one-factor construct and the different schemas are not merely specific skills but are manifestations of an underlying integrated structure of thought. Within certain limits set by the reliability of the tasks, it is possible from two or three samplings of a pupil's performance to characterise his/her capacity in terms of the level at which he/she presently functions. The experimental evidence offered here relates strictly to the utility of such a construct, in the sense of its ability to predict performance over a wide range of school science activities, as was shown in Chapter 5.

In conclusion, one might note that the difference between our view and that of Karplus and Lawson can be seen to be only a matter of quantitative emphasis. There is some specific variance associated with different combinations of schemas but there is much more common variance. It is this common variance which lies at the foundation of the case we present in this book.

NOTE

Because of the central nature of this chapter to our argument, the critical reader is urged to refer to [56] where much of the background detail and technical argument is presented in full. For a full account of the technical aspects of the treatment of data, and of the development of the tasks, the reader should consult [52].

Part 3

8 A curriculum analysis taxonomy

We have shown, especially in Chapters 5 and 6, how useful an estimation of the level of thinking demanded by science curriculum activities can be. Such a method of assessment can be used to select objectives and activities suitable for a given group of pupils, and also to rank levels of attainment within a topic such as heat or electricity according to the cognitive demand that they make. In this chapter we will take a closer look at this sort of analysis of curricula, and introduce a method which can be used by science teachers who have no specialised knowledge of Piagetian psychology.

We have already pointed to the inadequacy of Piaget's logical metatheory, both in terms of consistency and in its ability to make predictions which are empirically valid (pp. 26, 61, and 62). This places us in a difficult, but not insoluble, quandary. It is like being a chemist in the period after Mendeleev and before Bohr. If we had a satisfactory meta-model it would be possible to use it to analyse existing problems and to make economic predictions based on the model much in the way that, for example, the shapes of molecules and the numbers of bonds between atoms constituting them can be predicted using the quantum theory descriptions of atomic and molecular orbitals. In fact no such powerful metatheory exists but a descriptive model analogous to the periodic table has been shown, as was the periodic table itself in the hands of experienced chemists, to yield predictions which have a high level of empirical validity.

Constructing a curriculum analysis taxonomy

This is the background before which our work on curriculum analysis has been played out. It has led to the view that the best way to develop the skill of curriculum analysis lies not with making a premature attempt to construct a new overall theory to replace that of Piaget, but rather to use the very considerable structure of his work which has been further validated by the studies reported here. The schemas which he describes as underlying children's thinking are used as the basis for constructing a descriptive *taxonomy*. This taxonomy arranges and classifies objectives into groups according to (a) the schema or reasoning patterns employed, and (b) the stage of cognitive development of which they are character-istic.

The work of analysis of science curricula published in the early seventies [49] was based mainly on two levels of abstraction from *The Growth of Logical Thinking, The Child's Construction of Quantities, The Early Growth of Logic*, and other works. This method presupposed an intimate knowledge of those works of Piaget, and however well it may have worked in the hands of its author [50; 54], it would not constitute a method which could be used by most science teachers. It was necessary to develop a taxonomy which provided a detailed summary of the grounds of judgement which are scattered about the voluminous works of Piaget.

Essentially this method is to take a number of different aspects of think-ing sufficient to cover a wide range of science activities, but not so many that the user is confused by an embarrassment of choice. Two complemen-tary taxonomies are provided, the first dealing with six aspects, or cate-gories, and the second with nine categories, making fifteen grounds of judgement in all. These amount to a comprehensive definition of concrete and formal operational thinking in behavioural terms.

The first taxonomy describes psychological characteristics of children's thinking at each of five stages from pre-operational (stage 1) to late formal operational (stage 3B), most of which are relevant to the understanding of science although some extend more widely in their scope. Taxonomy 1 concentrates on the mental activities of the pupil; it is alternative and complementary to taxonomy 2.

The second taxonomy, while still described in terms of typical pupil responses, concentrates on the intellectual elements or schemas specific to different types of science activity. Thus proportionality and equilibrium of systems are involved in many aspects of physics and chemistry, whereas control of variables and correlational reasoning are more often used in biology.

The two taxonomies follow on pages 72-5 and 76-9.

Using the taxonomies

Experience during trials (detailed in Chapter 10) of this curriculum analysis shows that different raters generally agree about the level of demand of a curriculum activity, *provided that they agree about just what it is that they are rating.* Where the objectives, and the teaching method, are spelt out in detail in the teachers' guide there is less room for ambiguity, but in most cases the user must decide for himself what teaching methods he would use, and just what objectives are implied. Much curriculum material allows for more than one method of presentation, and more than one expected response from the pupil. The rating will depend on the presentation and expectations chosen.

Even given clearly specified objectives, there is no 'best route' through the taxonomies, and different users will choose different points of entry. Before you start, you might read again the general account of formal and concrete operational thinking given in Chapter 3 (pp. 26-9), and then read through all of taxonomies 1 and 2 to get an overview of the responses that you can expect at different stages.

Skill and speed in curriculum analysis comes, we have found, by learning to spot which of the categories are appropriate for the objectives being assessed. This is best learnt by attempting to assess a varied set of objectives from different sciences and of differing difficulty, taken from curricula familiar to the reader. If for each objective the attempt is made to use *two* of the taxonomy 1 categories, and *two* of the taxonomy 2 categories in order to arrive at an assessment, this will ensure that the different aspects of the objective are all borne in mind before an overall judgement is made. A quick search through the six categories in taxonomy 1 and the nine categories in taxonomy 2 will suggest which of the behavioural descriptions apply, and practice with particular cases soon leads to a 'feel' for the categories to look for. Moreover, the first four categories in taxonomy 2 were written with the physical sciences in mind, and the last five mainly for biological and social sciences.

To provide the opportunity for such practice, we give on p. 80 some illustrations of the use of the taxonomies, and in the following chapter some sets of examples from biology, chemistry, and physics. Indeed, the best introduction to curriculum analysis may well be through examples from your specialist subject given in Chapter 9.

You will probably find that rating is slow at first, but it becomes much faster as you become familiar with the taxonomy material. But however accomplished you feel that you have become in rating curricula, you should

Table 8.1   *Taxonomy 1:* Different aspects of the development of the child's interaction with the world.

Function	1 pre-operational	2A early concrete	2B late concrete
1.1 Interest and Investigation style	Things are believed to be exactly as they appear to immediate perception. Perception dictates decisions. Faced with a mature person's idea of evidence, will deny it, explain it anthropomorphically, or be silent. Does not perceive contradictions.	Will register what happens, but for interest to be maintained after the first obvious observations needs a seriative or simple associative model[4]. Unaided investigation style does not go as far as producing concrete models. (see 1.4—2A and 2B)	Will include seriation [1] and classification [2] as tools of perception in finding out what happens, but needs to be provided with a concrete model by which to structure experimental results (classes must be given, and examples of the application shown). Finds interest in making and checking cause-and-effect predictions.
1.2 Reasons for events	Interprets phenomena egocentrically, in terms of his own self.	See 1.1, 1.3, and 1.4: 'Cause-and-effect only partly structured— 'this goes with that'; so uses associative reasoning. Simple one-factor causes, such as 'force', etc.	Bipolar concepts such as 'alkali destroys acid'. Can use ordering relationships to partially quantify associative relationships: 'as this goes up, that goes down', 'if you double this you must double that', i.e. 'the reason' involves describing the relationship or categories, not providing a formal model. Cause-and-effect structured according to general concrete stage schemas as 'adding acid makes the pH lower'.
1.3 Relationships	Cannot consistently arrange data in an ordered series.	Can order a series, but is unlikely to see that as an obvious way of summing up observations. Nominal scale[3] relationships—'same distance—same weight' (See-Saw).	Can multiply seriations, and hence can find 1:1 correspondence between two sets of readings (e.g. weights and extensions of springs), and hence any linear relationship. Readily uses the notion of reversibility. Will use compensation argument to explain a conservation where only *ONE* variable is independent, e.g. of a piece of clay 'you've made it longer, but it's thinner so its the same'. See also 2.2.

[1] Seriation: putting objects or data into order according to a property such as length, mass (ordinal scales).
[2] Classification : putting things in groups according to common property.

3A early formal	*3B late formal*
Finds further interest in beginning to look for *why*, and following out consequences from a formal model. Confused by the request to investigate empirical relationships without an interpretative model. Can use a formal model, (see 1.4—3A) but requires it to be provided. Can generate concrete models with interest. Can see the point of making hypotheses, and can plan simple controlled experiments, but is likely to need help in deducing relationships from results and in organising the information so that irrelevant variables are excluded at each step.	Finds interest in generating and checking possible 'why' explanations. Will tolerate absence of an interpretative model while investigating empirical relationships. Takes it as obvious that in a system with several variables he must 'hold all other things equal' while varying one at a time, and can plan such investigations and interpret results. Will make quantitative checks involving proportionality relationships.
Looks for some causative necessity behind a relation established with concrete schemas. Allows for the possibility of a cause that is not in 1:1 correspondence with observations. Can consider the possibility of multiple causes for one effect, or multiple effects of one cause. Can suspend judgement and allow results of controlled experiments to constrain choice among various cause-and-effect explanations. Can handle formal models as explanatory provided their structure is simple (see 1.4).	Because aware of multiple causes and effects can think of reality in a multivariate way, so can make a general or abstract formulation of a relationship which covers all cases in an economical way. Can use deduction from the properties of a formal model—either from its mathematical or internal physical structure—to make explanatory predictions about reality.
Uses compensation relationships between TWO independent variables, e.g. weights and distances on both arms of a balance can be changed while preserving equilibrium; resistance is related to both area and length, in electricity. See also 2.2. Simple functional relationships beyond linear, and thus acceleration. (Note that this is a more sophisticated version of the concrete modelling described in 1.4(2B), rather than formal modelling.)	Can reflect upon reciprocal relationship between several variables. Thus can handle quantitative 'relations between relations' as in proportions, or semi-quantitative relationships as in chemical equilibria. This level of thinking is often needed for analysing experimental results so as to order them for lower-level computation, e.g. weight changes in reactions involving different elements and compounds, or density calculations where density is an inferred concept (density of gases, or Archimedes' problems). See 2.4—3B.

[3] Nominal Scale: scale with two values only: 'Four legs good: two legs bad'.
[4] Association: co-incidence in time or place serving as basis for prediction.

Function	1 pre-operational	2A early concrete
1.4 Use of Models	Not possible	*Concrete modelling* is the organisation of reality by seriation or classification or 1:1 correspondence. At this level simple comparisons only, and elementary causes—'*this* opposes *that*'. Unstructured notions such as 'pureness'.
1.5 Type of Categorisation	Thought is associational, and association of one aspect (e.g. height) not linked to another aspect (e.g. breadth) on anything but an immediate perceptual or temporary basis. Thus has difficulty classifying objects into even two groups as successive judgements on one object are contradictory.	Elementary classification. Sets of objects are classified according to one major criterion at a time, e.g. colour, size, shape, etc. Children can also switch criteria. Soon they can also multiply classifications, i.e. 'big blue squares/small blue squares', 'red big squares /red small squares'.
1.6 Depth of Interpretation(of descriptive passages)	Does not look for contradictions in interpreting a descriptive account. Tends to pick on one feature only.	Imposes a consistent interpretation, but builds it around one feature of the account. Nominal scale [3] level of interpretation.

2B late concrete	3A early formal	3B late formal
Modelling by seriation extends to any linear scale. For classification see 1.5—2B. For 'cause-and-effect' see 1.2 and 1.3. 'Model' now has dictionary definition of simplified 1:1 correspondence model (skeleton; gearbox, etc.).	*Formal modelling* is the indirect interpretation of reality by deductive comparison from a postulated system with its own rules. At this level student usually needs guidance in deducing how a system with several variables may behave. Unless quantitative relationship is simple (as with 'caloric' model of heat transfer, or 'pressure' as F/A) deduction is likely to be qualitative only (exchange reactions with metals and oxides). Model is taken as true, not hypothesis, so this level does not allow critical comparison of alternative formal models.	Can actively search for an explanatory model, extend one that is given, and compare alternative models for how they account for the same data. Since proportional thinking is readily available (relating two independent variables to each other) can formulate quantitative deductions from the model, and reflect on the relations between the variables.
Class inclusion and hierarchical classification. Classification is still the dominant mode of categorising reality, but now the classes are less tied to one simple property, and can also be partially ordered, e.g. animals – flying animals – domestic birds. Bi-polar classifications such as 'Acids and Alkalis as opposites'.	Generalisation. Now the classifying operation is used to impose meaning over a wide range of phenomena. A general formula like $V = hlb$ will be used as an instruction for computing volume. Asked to choose the next term in the series 'Etna—volcano—...' would pick 'mountain' as the best classifier.	Abstraction. By contrast, would prefer 'geological notion' to 'mountain' as next stage of categorisation. Because of the multivariate nature of reality it is sometimes more powerful to search among the many properties for the essence of the underlying association. Mountain is a higher class, but geological notion abstracts so that connections with non-mountains can be explored. In $V = hlb$, the way in which h and b vary in relation to one another for constant l and V.
Takes several aspects of described situation into account, but separately, and in imposing cause-effects stays within the descriptions, and mostly redescribes it. Ordinal scale ([2]) level of interpretation. (Examine whether a concrete model (1.4—2A and 2B) is provided.)	Extended describer level. Still stays largely within the descriptive account, but considers more than one aspect at once (trees removed; rain on soil; soil washed away).	Explainer thinking. Not only are all the relevant features of the description accounted for, but hypotheses are tested against the data and, when necessary, inferences made imaginatively using outside ideas and data. (Examine whether a formal model (1.4—3A and 3B) is provided as an interpretation.)

Table 8.2   *Taxonomy 2:* The development of different 'schemas' required for the understanding of the sciences.

Type of problem	2A early concrete	2B late concrete
2.1 Conservation	Accepts that the amount of substance does not change, but still believes that weight and volume do, except in the very simplest situations, e.g. accepts volume constant when liquid poured to different shaped vessel, but volume of water displaced does not equal volume of displacing body. Conserves number and length.	Conservation of weight even when the dimensions of the body are changed. Volume conserved if body can be seen, but not if it dissolves.
2.2 Proportionality	Can double or halve the quantity of two related sets, e.g. if 2 oranges cost 4p, one orange costs 2p.	Has not arrived at metric proportions[1]. Can make inferences from data involving constant ratio, so long as ratio is a small whole number, e.g. if 2 sweets cost 5p, 6 will cost 15p. Thus can scale up by factors of two or three, and partition using simple whole numbers.
2.3 Equilibria of systems	See 1.3—2A. Observations ordered in terms of one property.	Relationships between variables only conceptualised two at a time, with the relationship linear (direct or inverse). (Single variables like force not compound variables such as pressure.)
2.4 Mathematical Operations	Number is now distinguished effectively from size, shape, appearance. Number as a series, but confined to the numbers which can be given a conceivable concrete realisation.	Can work with single operations (e.g. addition, subtraction, division and multiplication) but the system of numbers must have *closure*; i.e. the operation must be unambiguous and the result of the operation must be within the set, e.g. $5 + 4 = x$ can be solved, but $? - 7 = 7 - 3$ or $5 \div 4$ cannot.

[1] Metric proportions. The equivalence of two numerical ratios e.g. $2/6 = 7/21$.

3A early formal	3B late formal
All conservations. Now understands how the volume of odd-shaped objects can be determined by displacement. Notion of pure substance, which is conserved even when mixed with other (pure) substances. Realises that the volume of liquid displaced by a body does *not* depend on its weight.	

3A early formal	3B late formal
Can make inferences where a ratio of simple whole numbers is involved, e.g. if a 2 kg box costs 12p and a 3 kg box costs 15p, which is the best buy? Can handle, as functional relation-ships, ratio variables such as density as weight/volume; current/voltage, and gas volume changes with temperature and pressure. $n_1v_1 = n_2v_2$ in chemical volumetric work.	Can formulate and quantify relationships between different ratio concepts mentioned under 3A descriptions, e.g. in investigating the shadows cast by different sized rings, 'the ratio between the ring sizes and the distances has to be the same'. Think-ing in terms of direct or inverse relations between ratio variables (e.g. moles/litre, or mass/ atomic mass) knows how to model the relationships mathematically. See 2.4—3B. In volumetric work can handle computation in terms of V_2/V_1, *therefore C_1/C_2.*
Where there are two independent vari-ables related to each other at equilib-rium, will discover this relationship, provided the ratios are simple whole numbers e.g. 3/2; 1/4; 3/4, etc. e.g. $W_1/W_2 = L_2/L_1$ in a balance, or $h_1/h_2 = a_2/a_1$ in hydraulic press, without grasping the internal law of the whole system.	Can compare any ratio in two independent vari-ables' equilibria by treating them as a proportion. When there are 3 or more variables related to each other at equilibrium, can conceptualise the relationship of the third to the other two, and thus arrive at a general law for the system, and can discuss the reciprocal relation of the first two variables e.g. in the case of the inclined plane relates the truck weight and hanging weight variables by equating them to the ratio of the vertical rises and fall of each. Can provide an *explanation* for a relation established at 3A level, e.g. $h_1/h_2 = a_2/a_1$, because pressure produced by each arm is the same—leading to view of the whole system.
Concrete generalisation. Can work with the relationship $V = lbh$ or $W_1H_1 = W_2H_2$ but only by treating each step as a definite operation on definite numbers. Begins to accept lack of closure, e.g. can solve $? - 7 = 7 - 3$ by a series of operations to each side of the relation.	Can properly conceive of a *variable*, and begins to work with the explicit rules of a system so as to develop proof strategies. See 1.3—3B. Rather than needing a formula where several variables are involved, can analyse the set of relations required by the model so as to sequence correctly a series of simple computations e.g. with a 'hydrogen– oxygen' model realises the weight changes relating to H and O separately must be computed before weights of other com-pounds can be computed. Before a density calcula-tion can be set up the relevant weight and volume changes must be found.

Type of problem	*2A early concrete*	*2B late concrete*
2.5 Control of variables	Can reject a proposed experimental test where a factor whose effect is intuitively obvious is un-controlled, at the level of 'that's not fair', but fails to separate variables and so eliminate one. 'Fairness' may also be applied in the sense of giving every factor an equal chance, e.g. 'Slower runner should be given shorter distance'.	Will usually vary more than one factor in each experiment, and often varies other factors to test the effect of a given one.
2.6 Exclusion of Variables	In analysis of a multivariate problem (e.g. pendulum, flexibility of rods of different materials, shape, etc.) has no strategy for excluding interfering variables. May attempt to order the effects of factors and may arrive at the direction of the effects if they are intuitively obvious, e.g. 'longer rods bend more'.	Will order the effects of a given factor, but fails to exclude the interference of the other factors because he is trying to impose bivariate thinking. Thus often arrives at correct effect of a factor by invalid arguments. Unlikely to arrive at correct effect where it is contrary to intuition or where the factor makes no difference.
2.7 Probabalistic Thinking	No notions of probability.	Given 3 red objects and 3 yellow objects mixed up in bag, realises that there is a 50/50 chance of drawing a red one.
2.8 Correlational Reasoning		No systematic method of estimating the strength of a relationship except to look to see if the confirming cases are bigger in number than all the rest.
2.9 Measurement Skills	Makes measurements by comparing beginning and ending of object/journey with rule in simple whole numbers.	Bar diagrams, histograms, idea of *mean* as the centre of a histogram, and variation as its breadth. Graphical relationships of first order equations. Interpretation of graphs where there is a 1:1 correspondence with the object modelled, e.g. height/time relationship for the growth of a plant.

3A early formal	*3B late formal*
Sees the need to vary one factor at a time and can suggest experimental tests to control for factors explicitly named. May fail to control factors that are not perceptually obvious. Fails to develop a strategy based on a feeling of the system as a whole. May not see the point of having an experiment without a factor present to see if it is a variable.	Sets up suitable experiments to economically control factors and eliminate ones that are not effective, and can apply 'all other things equal' strategy to multivariable problems. More sophisticated biological experiments possible including interaction effects. Appreciates the impossibility of controlling natural variation, and so the need for proper sampling.
Will correctly arrive at the effect of a factor from experiments in which he/she has controlled for the other factors, but will often fail to exclude the effect of other factors when asked to select, from a group of experiments, those required to show the effect of each factor. Thus when two factors have been changed, and an effect is noticed, is likely to attribute change to the combination of both.	Because of an implicit knowledge of the different effects which may be caused by the combinations of the variables that are possible will select economically from a variety of experiments those required to show the effect or non effect of each in turn.
Given other ratios of objects will count the numbers of the given type (n) and the number of all objects (N) and express the chance of selection as a fraction n/N.	
Begins to look at the ratio of confirming to disconfirming cases, but tends to look only at the probability of two of the four cases, e.g. for blue or brown eyes and light or dark hair will compare the ratio of those with blue eyes and blond hair to those with blue and dark.	Realises that the opposite pairs are as important as each other. Thus takes the brown eyes/dark hair set together with the blue eyes/fair hair set, and compares it with the sum of the two disconfirming cases (brown/fair and blue/dark).
Interpretation of higher order graphical relations, and use of problem-solving algorithms, e.g. $P_1V_1 = P_2V_2$ for gas pressure calculations. Can make interpretations which involve relations *between* variables in a graph, e.g. in a distance/time graph will see that a vertical section means 'standing still' and that a horizontal section is impossible.	Interpretation of higher order graphical relations in terms of *rates* (instantaneous slopes) and reciprocal relationships; conceptualisation of relationships between variables, e.g. in $V=lbh$, if l rises (V constant), b and/or h must drop proportionally.

always refer back to the taxonomies from time to time to check against 'drifting' away from the criteria described there.

Familiarity with the taxonomies gained from a case-study approach will lead to an understanding of the underlying unifying theory, which emerges as a professional skill. It is one of the key-points of this book that such a skill should become part of the repertory of all science educators whether their field is primary, secondary, or even tertiary education.

ILLUSTRATIONS

1 In a comparison of plastic and non-plastic objects, a teachers' guide suggests that pupils should drop the same weight from an increasing height on to an egg box, and note the damage caused.

If pupils were simply given the problem 'compare the effects of falling weights on different egg boxes', and left to devise their own experiment, then this would involve formal operational thinking (3A by 2.5 and 1.1). However the context of this activity which comes from LAMP (28) suggests that the teacher will set up and direct the experiment. Simply to follow instructions, and even to record results, does not require cognitive processing above stage 1, but for the activity to have any purpose, the pupil must order his results in a series. If the teacher (or a worksheet) sets this up, the demand level would be 2A, by 1.3. The late concrete (2B) pupil would be likely to put the results in order without such guidance (1.1).

2 In an investigation into the factors that affect the movement of a pond organism, *Daphnia*, the teacher adds carbon dioxide to a jar containing *Daphnia*, and they crowd to the surface. Association alone (1.2) is not sufficient here, since we are looking for cause-effect relations. For the simple conclusion that carbon dioxide causes the *Daphnia* to surface, late concrete operations are sufficient (2B, 1.2), since cause and effect are directly observable.

However the next steps in the same activity involve the *interaction* of light and carbon dioxide as variables, the implied association of extra carbon dioxide with depletion of oxygen, and the relation of the conclusions to the advantages to *Daphnia* of this behaviour in its pond life. Even when the experiments are set up by the teacher, the pupil must appreciate interaction effects (3B by 2.5) and cope with relations between relations (3B by 1.3).

It is hard to see how this activity could serve any purpose at a lower level of demand, unless the object was simply to impress on pupils that 'the behaviour of organisms is very complicated'.

3 In an investigation of limestone, pupils shake some with water, and then are asked

(i) Does it dissolve?

(ii) How could you find out if any has dissolved?

The first question depends on the pupils' comprehension of the word 'dissolve'. Even at 2A, it is possible for pupils to establish association of the word 'dissolve' with the observation of a solid disappearing to form a clear solution (1.2, 1.5). This seems to be all that is required for a 'no' answer.

The second question is more difficult. A child who can mentally reverse the process (2B by 1.3) could learn and understand a technique for recovering a dissolved solid from a solution. But here he can *see* undissolved solid; must *imagine* that some could have dissolved (i.e. must see the point of the hypothesis that some could have dissolved, 3A by 1.1); and must search his repertory of separation techniques to synthesise a suitable method. This could be seen as requiring the use of a model of solution (3A by 1.4), and the problem would be rated as demanding early formal operational thinking, at least when it is presented as a novel situation. This is not to say that testing to see if some has dissolved could not be learned as a rote technique at the concrete level, but the context of this activity suggests that this technique has not been learned.

A TRAINING-EXERCISE IN THE USE OF THE TAXONOMIES

Using the examples below, you can compare your rating of some published science curriculum activities with that of the CAT's compilers. Two examples from each of the three sciences are given, and the objectives spelled out to reduce ambiguity. Attempts to rate each objective, and to list the taxonomy category numbers you use, and the level of description within each category that seems to correspond best with the objective. Our own responses are given at the end of the chapter.

Reference		*Objective*
O level		
(1) Nuffield Chemistry	Exp.11.4(c)	To use the experimental result and by
The Sample Scheme	p. 239–241	calculation to realise that the atom
Stages I and II		ratio in water is 2:1
Revised Teachers		
Guide I	p. 63–5	
(2) Revised Teachers	Exp.13.3(a)	After putting chlorine, bromine, and
Guide II	p. 95–7	iodine in reactivity order (a 2B objective) to relate this trend to the position of the halogens in the periodic table.
O level		
(3) Nuffield Physics	Exps.60, 61	To interpret the two experiments as
Guides to	p. 162–168	meaning that bromine diffuses slower
Experiments		in air.
Revised Teachers	p. 167–8	
Guide III		
(4)		To interpret the experiments as showing that the diffusion into a vacuum shows the true rate of movement of the bromine molecules.

(5)	Nuffield Combined Science Teachers Guide II	6-3c p.36–37	By comparing two cans alongside each other to realise that the one covered with feathers cools down slower.
(6)		To carry out own experiments as suggested so as to realise that surface area is an important variable.

SCIS (Rand McNally (1970) edition):

(7)	Teachers' Guide, Interactions & Systems Part 4, pp. 64–69	To use the word *system* to refer to a group of related objects. To *predict* the relative turning rates of interacting pulleys
(8)		(a) when circumferences are in a 2:1 ratio.
(9)		(b) when circumferences are in a 6:1 ratio.
(10)	SCIS: Environments TG, Chapter 11, pp. 70–73	To record growth of different plants on chart provided.
(11)		To conclude that light affects rate of plant growth.
(12)		To describe qualitatively different effect of light on different plants.
(13)	CHEMstudy TG, p. 24.	To obtain cooling curve for liquid as it solidifies.
(14)		To interpret flat zone as 'heat still given off while temperature remains constant'.
(15)	ASEP Metals (Teachers' Edition) Option 8, Modifying metal properties	To learn what is the effect of 'working' metal. (p. 94)
(16)		To link work-hardening with grain structure. (p. 95)
(17)		To interpret grain boundary and deformation in terms of ions, from the bubble-raft analogy. (pp. 99, 100)

NOTE

The consultative committee involved in the development of the taxonomies given in this chapter are shown in session in the photograph at the beginning of Part 3. They were Bob Allen, Chris Butlin, David Charles, Gill Crowther, John Deadman, Andrew Firman, Jeff Moore, Mike Newman, and John Oxley.

CLASSIFICATION OF OBJECTIVES BY COMPILERS OF CAT

(1) 1.3(3B); 2.2(3B); 2.3(3B)
(2) 1.1(3A); 1.4(3A); 2.3(3A)
(3) 1.1(2B); 1.2(2B); 2.3(2B)
(4) 1.1(3A); 1.4(3A); 1.2(3A)
(5) 1.2(2A); 1.6(2A); 2.5(2A)
(6) 1.1(3A); 1.2(3A); 1.6(3A); 2.5(3A)
(7) 1.6(2A); 1.5(2A); 1.4(2A)
(8) 2.2(2B); 2.3(2B); 1.2(2B);
(9) 2.2(3A); 2.3(3a); 1.2(2B) or (3A) depending if 'much faster' or '6 times'
(10) 1.5(1); 2.4(2A)
(11) (2A) by 1.2, 1.3, 2.5 and 2.6.
(12) 2B by 1.3, 1.6. and by not requiring 3A criteria in 2.5, 2.6.
(13) 2B by 1.1, 1.2, 2.3 and 2.9
(14) 3A by 1.1, 1.4, 2.3, 2.9
(15) 2A by 1.1, 1.2 & 1.4
(16) concrete modelling—2B by 1.1, 1.4,
(17) formal modelling—3A by 1.1, 1.2, 1.4.

9 Objectives in the sciences

In this chapter the process of curriculum analysis is applied to the traditional modes of teaching physics, chemistry, and biology in order to delineate the implicit hierarchy involved in familiar routines. It is hoped that this will be particularly useful for the subject specialist—whether he or she be a university consultant or secondary teacher in love with his science —in thinking about the extent to which traditional aims can be modified to suit a wider range of pupil.

Each of the three sciences traditionally taught in schools has developed sets of routines, which amount to well-recognised 'games'—games with rules (explicit and implicit) which the student must learn in order to be deemed successful. Often teachers themselves are not fully aware of this. For instance, the differences between the games of school chemistry, of university chemistry (which an academic remembers as 'real' chemistry), of industrial chemistry (whch an employer may expect students to have started on), and of social chemistry (which the theoretical educator may expect from science education in school) are not clearly recognised. The purpose of this book is to give some assistance to teachers of sciences, especially in schools, in recognising and understanding some of the sources of difficulty of science to pupils. Thus we concentrate in this chapter on the rules of some of the games in biology, chemistry, and physics as they are played in school. Games such as 'biological controls', 'physical and chemical change', 'kinetic and potential energy', must be played and won to pass school examinations, and because of their importance in schools and school curricula they are the ones that are analysed in this book. In the process of developing new ideas of school science it will be helpful to see how the rules of the 'games' have been developed to suit the selective school pupils who have traditionally been their players.

Overview: a note on the major differences between the sciences

Whatever may be the merits or demerits of thinking about science as a whole, as suggested in the ASE discussion document *Alternatives for Science Education* [1], it is useful to be able to describe the differences between the three traditional sciences, and the differences in approach which these necessitate.

For different reasons, both physics and biology are accessible, in some aspects, at lower levels of conceptual demand than is chemistry. In the case of physics this is because many law-like behaviours are simple bivariate functions involving only one independent variable, which are linear in form. Examples are Hooke's law, relating the extension of a spring to the applied load, and the relationship, for a given circuit, of the current flow rising linearly with applied voltage. Also many describable variables, like force or temperature, have an inner logic which is modelled by concrete operational schemas (see Chapter 8—taxonomy 1.4). In biology much descriptive zoology and botany involves no experimental design, and involves little application of mathematical modelling beyond notions of central values (averages) and variation (ranges) which form part of the content of modern maths courses in late primary and early secondary schooling.

Chemistry, by contrast, cannot be said to begin in 'recognisable form'[1] [3] (to quote Bruner's well-known statement) until the pupil has some notion of a *compound* in which the masses of its constituent elements are retained even though all their other properties are lost. Since it can readily be seen, by a number of criteria in taxonomy 1, that this requires a minimum of early formal (3A) thinking it follows that this 'idea or problem or body of knowledge' *cannot* 'be presented in a form simple enough so that any particular learner can understand it'. Since the first act of chemistry involves formal modelling, this science has a high 'entrance fee' compared with the other two traditional sciences. On the other hand a considerable body of descriptive chemistry can be learnt without involving any higher level of cognitive demand.

Yet both physics and biology are *more* demanding when it comes to grasping the great integrating ideas which must to some extent be mastered before the pupil can feel either that he or she is more than a beginning student, or that he/she has some notion of the subject-matter of the science as forming a single and particular way of viewing the world. Again the reasons are different. In physics the system of Newton's Laws, the laws of equilibrium of physical systems, and the way in which elementary thermodynamics links a number of apparently contradictory aspects of energy all involve comparatively complex mathematical modelling of systems with several independent variables. But, by contrast to biology, the variables themselves are usually simple and amenable to physical intuition. In biology the great notions of community and ecosystem, of cell function, of genetics and evolution, and homeostasis, do perhaps fall under Bruner's description. Yet the difficulty in biology is in rooting any of the great notions in a sufficient quantity of structured knowledge so that they begin to perform a substantial amount of integrating work. The complexity of thought required for competence is qualitatively different—though equivalent — between the two sciences. (Incidentally this difference, if it could be adequately described, may possibly help to explain sex-differentials in mastering physics and biology.)

The 'games' of physics

Before the game of physics can be played, a number of smaller 'games' must be learnt. At an abstract level, these can be described as

(a) the concrete bivariate relationships
(b) the relationships involving intuitive qualitative and semi-quantitative models (kinetic theory, fluid model of electricity, etc.)
(c) relationships involving ratio variables like $P = F/A$ and simple first order functions involving two independent variables, such as a capacity/potential pair, with a qualitative model of the capacity factor
(d) equilibria of physical systems
(e) integrated postulatory and deductive systems (Newton's Laws, elementary thermodynamics, and the First Law of Thermodynamics)
(f) further integration of the systems in (e) with each other.

This series forms a psychological hierarchy. The problem in teaching and learning physics is that many of the phenomena covered in (a), (b), and (c) have to be studied separately, and apparently in isolation, before the integrating steps (e) and (f) begin to draw the subject together into a unity. In Piagetian terms (a) involves 2B thinking, (b) and (c) involve 3A, (d) is intermediate, and (e) and (f) both require late formal (3B) thinking.

If physics is taught to students of university age, and possessing 3B competence, then the curriculum planner has freedom of choice as to whether the separate aspects of the science are taught separately at a low level first, or whether, from the outset, an Ausubelian strategy of 'advance organisers' is used to promote an integrated understanding so that the separate 'games' are set in their context at the same time as experience is gained of them. But if the curriculum developer is planning a course for schoolchildren involving the subject-matter of physics, where the children may be any age from 9 to 16 (to cover the range which is relevant in Britain) his choice is constrained by the level of cognitive development of the pupils as it changes year by year. The (intellectually) very beautiful course, Nuffield O level Physics is seen to be suitable only for the top 5 per cent of 11 to 16 year-old secondary school pupils if its lesson-sequences are compared with the developmental data featured in Chapter 2 (Figure 2.5). The parallel PSSC course in the USA, because it is taught only to the 16–18 year-olds, is a little less constrained, but assuming similar population norms is still available only to the top 12–13 per cent.

Since the amount of information in individual science topics is considerable, it will be convenient if the descriptions are tabulated in a mode similar to that employed for the curriculum-analysing taxonomy. Where it may be helpful, an indication is given of how the steps fit the hierarchy just mentioned. If the columns for the 2B, 3A, and 3B descriptions in Table 9.1 are scanned from the aspect of the mathematics involved, it will be seen that, in comparison with the other two sciences, growth in competence in physics demands the parallel growth of skill in a particular kind of mathematical modelling. One might say that learning physics is to a large extent developing this skill until it is almost second nature as an approach to modelling the world. It will also be noticed that while 3A thinking gives access to this skill at an executive level, as may be required for some forms of technical education, the kind of skill aimed at unremittingly by the Nuffield O level physics course is that described in the 3B columns.

Table 9.1 *Physics.*

Topic	2A *early concrete*	2B *late concrete*
P.1 Floating and Sinking Density	At this level Mass, Weight, Volume, and Density are still 'collapsed' in a global notion of 'heaviness'; knows that wood will float, iron will sink, but without a general explanation available, he can only learn a series of individual facts about materials.	Specific theories of floating will be tested, and weight differentiated from mass as a variable. Volume will only partly be conceptualised, and so the weight/volume relationship will not yet be used as an explanatory tool. Different 'heaviness' of materials will be differentiated from 'bigness'. 'A small or a large piece of plasticine will both sink, because the stuff is the same, with the same heaviness.'
P.2 Force and Pressure	Pressure = Force. 'Stiletto-heel' effect. i.e. The effect of a force is greater if it acts through a thinner surface. 'Force' is a concept which is ordered—'*this* bigger than *that*'	Force in liquids is greater at greater depth. Vacuum is treated as a negative force. Air exerts a global force. Force can be partitioned, e.g. where 1 kg weight is lowered on to different numbers of 1 cm^3 blocks. The word 'pressure' may be used, but still given a working definition of 'force'.
P.3 Equilibrium of Physical Systems	Nominal equilibrium relationships, e.g. at ends of a see-saw in balance, both weights are the same. A smaller weight is more effective further from centre. To make a truck run down hill, put weight in it.	Produces an account of equilibrium in terms of bi-variate linear relationships. For a beam to balance, the heavier the weight the closer it must be to the centre. Likely to predict that halving the distance will compensate for doubling the weight. In the case of an inclined plane, can arrive at formulations like 'the greater the angle the more weight that is needed to stop a truck running down'.
P.4 Momentum	Intuitive, global concept of the relative impetus of colliding bodies. Can make predictions with some success which imply that the speed and mass are 'allowed for', i.e. slower and heavier can balance faster and lighter.	Differentiation of velocity from mass as contributory components of momentum, i.e. has a *language* with which to talk about predictions.
P.5 Velocity and Acceleration	Intuitive notion of speed, but speed and relative position not differentiated, thus likely to call that one faster which ends up ahead.	Speed as relating distances and time (feet per second; m.p.h.)—hence speeds compared by distance travelled in same time. Intuitive notion of acceleration.

3A early formal	*3B late formal*
Volume conceptualised and displacement seen to be a function of volume, not weight. Weight/volume relationship will be utilised to generate hypotheses in the floating/sinking problem. Complete solution including density of liquid unlikely to be discovered, but rules about relative density can be learned. 'You can find out if two things are the same substance by seeing if their weight/ volume ratio is the same.'	Can handle relationship between, say, density, mass, and spacing of particles. Could formulate a theory of floating relating density of solid to density of liquid, or is likely to find that the clue to the floating and sinking problem is the weight of displaced liquid.
Distinguishes force from pressure. Pressure is treated as force per unit area. The pressure in a gas or liquid is the same in all directions.	Can apply the pressure concept to the general understanding of conditions of equilibrium, e.g. in a hydraulic press, or water standing at the same height in two interconnecting tubes of different cross-sectional area.
If a system has *two* independent variables may find effect of each by a control of variables strategy. Can find equilibrium relationships where simple linear proportionality is involved, i.e. in a balance, given weights in 3:2 ratio will predict lengths from centre should be in 2:3 ratio. Can generalise to $L_1 W_1 = L_2 W_2$. For a given angle, in the inclined plane problem, will discover the relative weights as a proportion.	Quickly arrives at a proportionality formulation which can be tested as a hypothesis. Can generalise equilibria such as those of a balance in terms of a *work* principle (dynamic compensation of more force by less distance). Thus in the more complex inclined plane problem can test and discard a 'more weight/less angle' hypothesis and arrive at the quantitative solution.
Can use formula to calculate results of collisions when it is taught as an algorithm; i.e. as a procedure, together with elementary rules for the context of its application. Will realise that changes in momentum are caused by forces.	Reinterprets global concept of momentum in an analytical way. Deals with reciprocal relationship of mass and velocity, and can deal with Newton's first law as a conservation statement.
Acceleration conceived as rate of change of velocity. Thus 'ticker-tape' experiments on inclined plane begin to make sense. Can use second-power equations involving constant acceleration as a taught algorithm. ($S = ut + \frac{1}{2}at^2$)	Acceleration as the limiting value of $$\frac{\Delta v}{\Delta t}$$

	Topic	2A *early concrete*	2B *late concrete*
P.6	Newton's Laws	See P4, P5 and P2.	See P4, P5, and P2.
P.7	Electricity	Bulbs light when connected to batteries. A bright bulb has more energy than a dim bulb. Likely to internalise a 'one connection' model of electricity flow. No potential/current distribution.	Can use voltage as a global measure of electrical forces. Although readings on an ammeter are used, as a measure of electricity, concept of current tends to be collapsed under voltage, so effects of current are given a 'voltage' explanation.
P.8	Temperature and Heat	No distinction between heat and temperature. Temperature as a qualitative concept of hotness and coldness.	Temperature quite well conceptualised as linear 1:1 mapping of the number line on to 'degree of hotness'. Amount of heat only imperfectly conceptualised—usually collapsed under temperature. Amount of heat depends on mass of hot substance.
P.9	Kinetic Theory		See Tax.1.4. In no way is kinetic theory concrete modelling.
P.10	Energy and Power		Work is expended energy Energy has many sources Power *can* be differentiated from work All three concepts are intuitive and anthropomorphic
P.11	Thermodynamics		
P.12	Light		Can use a linear propagation (straight line) model to 'explain' reflection of seen rays from a flat mirror. 'The smaller the angle it goes in, the smaller the angle it goes out.' Shadows larger the nearer the object is to the light.

3A early formal	*3B late formal*
See P.4 for First Law. Where accelerations are constant can handle Second Law as a relationship between Force, Mass, and Acceleration. Unlikely to grasp the necessity for the Third Law, but can see the sense of it when confronted with experimental evidence.	See P.4 for First Law. Can analyse problems to see how to apply the first two Laws, and plan sequence of computations. Since he tends to think in terms of proof strategies can *eventually* see (from many examples) the necessity for the Third Law, and will treat all three as a set of axioms which produces consistent results.
Notion of resistance as V/I ratio. Can use a fluid model of current flow and predict with it properties of circuits, e.g. where direction of some of the batteries are changed, or where series is changed to parallel. Draws circuits in terms of a consistent two-connection model—e.g. will realise that a light-bulb must have a second connecting point for the filament.	Potential as an intensive property is distinguished from the extensive property of electricity, and hence potential as work required to transfer charge between two points. Potential drop in different parts of a complex circuit may be modelled (still needs to be taught well!).
Caloric model of heat/temperature relationship, and calculations involved. Kinetic theory picture accepted as providing explanation of particular phenomena, but not integrated with heat/temperature model.	Can use kinetic theory as predictive and explanatory model. Therefore can begin to appreciate the First Law of thermodynamics, and can deal with thermal equilibria as dynamic and statistical.
Used to explain only phenomena in simple correspondence with model. e.g. expansion due to greater vibration of particles, so particles expand or take up more space. Solution seen as intermingling of particles, so volume of solute is conserved.	Can appreciate its use as a deductive model proceeding from simple postulates. Relative properties of gases, liquids, and solids explained. Relative diffusion rates of different gases, and of gases into a vacuum compared with into air. Ready to appreciate quantitative derivation of gas laws and to conceive of temperature as only the mean value of a wide range of kinetic energies.
Work as a Force × Distance product. Kinetic energy as defined as $\frac{1}{2}mv^2$—hence deduction about stopping distances of cars from different speeds. Electric energy as $V \times I \times t$ product. Power as work done in unit time. Heat energy as calories.	Equivalence of different energy forms having each a capacity (extensive) and a potential (intensive) aspect. Energy as a general product of extensive and intensive factor. Can begin to appreciate the problem of Heat as a form of energy is only partly convertible to work.
Conservation of energy as a learnt concept. Mechanical equivalent of Heat as a learnt fact.	Capable of seeing $dE = W - q$ as a *postulate* which connects measured quantities to a formal model which, like Newton's Laws, appears to yield consistent predictions. Thus can eventually see that Heat, as a form of energy, needs a *second* postulate to connect it with other forms of energy.
Can use the Lens Laws to deal with real images (linear propagation model) but as algorithm. Uncomfortable with wave model as phenomena of light too obliquely connected with properties of model. Wavelength/frequency relationship as a computation algorithm. Light as part of em spectrum.	Can use wave model to account qualitatively for diffraction/interference phenomena. Can see Lens Laws as a deductive system and can learn to compute within their rules. Transverse and Longitudinal waves and velocity of transmission relating wavelength and frequency. Em spectrum and frequency of waves related to properties of emitting resonator.

The 'games' of chemistry

In physics, for reasons detailed earlier, the study of different topics can be arbitrarily placed in a variety of sequences, since it is only when they have been studied in sufficient depth that the integrating steps can begin to operate. By contrast, in chemistry both historical practise and psychological demand dictate a well-established hierarchy of steps.

Some of the elementary separation methods and phenomena of acidity and alkalinity and oxidation and reduction serve traditionally as an introduction to chemical concepts. Where one changes gear and introduces seriously the idea of a 'compound' has always been a matter of judgement related to how much longer the interest of the pupils can be kept up without an interpretative model. Just how far one can go in this introductory phase is clear from a quick scan of the 2B columns in Table 9.2. The American Chemstudy [4] course skips the pre-compound phase altogether, and Nuffield O level chemistry brings in the compound-model somewhere in the first two years (stage I), according to the teacher's choice. The next step or plateau involves the use of the notions of elements, compounds, and equations relating their reactions to the descriptive chemistry of the main types of ionic compounds (stopping short of complex cations). At this point acid-base reactions are given an interpretation in terms of hydrogen and

Table 9.2 *Chemistry*

Topic	2A early concrete	2B late concrete
C.1 Solution	Salt/sugar 'dissolve' in water. Mass of solute (i.e. global idea of amount) is conserved; but volume is not. (For the pre-operational child, the solute simply 'disappears'.)	The process is reversible.
C.2 Changes of State/Kinetic Theory	A solid 'turns to water', a liquid 'turns to gas', as discrete bits of information.	Ice melts to water, water turns to steam: each process can go back again on cooling. Heat causes the melting, cooling causes the freezing. A simple kinetic theory picture of molecules close together or far apart, but not applied by translation to reality.

hydroxyl ions, and oxidation-reduction reactions are dealt with in terms of valency changes, and proportion of non-metallic content.

The next level of complexity will involve thinking about chemical changes in terms of energetics, and developing the model of compounds to distinguish bond-type and types of structures. From here on the chemist has reached the equivalent of level (e) or (f) described for physics on page 86. As with physics the sequence of teaching is arbitrary, in that a number of equally effective routes are now possible. Yet whatever sequence is used the teacher will always have the higher objective in mind of a more and more integrated understanding of the subject. A detailed examination of the 3A and 3B columns in Table 9.2 will indicate the likely cognitive restrictions on the choice of routes for any particular level of students—whether they be third year comprehensive pupils (13 +) or fifth-year selective school pupils in the top 15 per cent of the ability-range.

If the contents of Table 9.2 are now compared with the developmental data given in Chapter 2, it will be seen that, because of the distance between the levels at which different chemistry 'games' are played, there are inherent problems about the extension of chemistry teaching throughout the secondary school which no amount of rhetoric about the social benefits of mixed-ability teaching, or about elitism, can make disappear.

3A early formal	*3B late formal*
The particles intermingle, but stay 'the same', so that each conserves volume, weight, and chemical properties.	Saturation involves an equilibrium situation, with precipitation rate = solution rate.
Application of kinetic theory under guidance, to the realisation that all materials might exist as solids, liquids, and gases, depending on the state of their particles. Liquifying means that the particles move around faster so they can change their position. You can measure how much energy is needed to do this with, say, an immersion heater.	Now kinetic theory model will be used deductively e.g. to explain how the particles in steam can be far apart and yet the steam can easily be compressed. Melting and vapourisation are equilibrium processes. Latent heat is the energy required to overcome the potential barrier between liquid and vapour. Different potential barriers in different liquids may be compared by comparing equimolar quantities.

Topic	2A *early concrete*	2B *late concrete*
C.3 Speed of Reaction	The hotter one goes faster. The stronger one goes faster. The weak one is slowest.	If you double the strength, the reaction goes twice as fast. If you raise the temperature by 10°C it goes nearly twice as fast. If you break up the solid, the reaction goes faster because the liquid can get at it more.
C.4 Elements and Particle Theory	Simplest purification routines, but understood magically, not analytically. No real sense of meaning of element.	Pure substances and purification as learned routines. Element as substance which no one has been able to split into anything simpler. Can order properties of elements under guidance, and so grade 'families' of elements.
C.5 Compounds, reactions and their chemical representation	Names used, but only associatively. No content given to a chemical name, thus no representation possible.	Chemical combinations remembered, without general rules being appreciated. Composition of compounds as a kind of mnemonic, e.g. water is made from hydrogen and oxygen, and will produce hydrogen and oxygen. Word equations could be used to indicate a reversible reaction, such as heat on hydrated copper sulphate. But 'copper' in that name is used only as a label, so word equation is only a statement of fact.
C.6 Acids and Alkalis	'Acid' as name of substances with certain properties—litmus, attacks metals, sour taste, but only one at a time, the properties are not seen as defining characteristics.	Acids and bases as opposing factions. The pH scale as an interval scale of degrees of acidity. Neutralisation by equal quantities of acid and alkali, if teacher has set up equivalent solutions. If you double quantity of acid, *or* if you double its concentration you need twice as much alkali. Metal oxides are basic (alkaline), non-metal oxides are acidic.

3A early formal	*3B late formal*

It goes faster when you break up the solid because the surface area gets greater. From the graph you can see that the slope is getting less, so the speed is getting less. *That* part of *that* graph shows that *that* reaction is going faster than *this*. As the concentration falls off, so does the speed.

$1/t$ measures how fast the reaction is going, so the graph shows speed is proportional to concentration. If you double the concentration, you double the collision rate and so double the speed. If you double the concentration of two reactants, the speed goes up by a factor of 4. Temperature? The particles are going faster and so collide more often. They also collide harder, so more react, so small temperature rise can have high effect on rate. Half-life, growth and decay curves in radio-chemistry. Can set up and conduct investigation into variables that govern, say, rate of decomposition of hydrogen peroxide.

Atoms have a structure. Some atoms are the same as each other, others are different. Element as a substance of one kind of atom, on a simple model of 'all red beads'. Purity in a similar sense. Knowledge that 100 per cent purity unattainable, without appreciation of the scale or numbers involved. The periodic table as a collection of 'families'; appreciation of simpler examples of two-way gradation of properties.

Measures of purity, limits of purity. Appreciation of the relation between experimental evidence and the various models of the atom. Oil drop experiment for the length of fatty acid molecules. The periodic table as a complex classificatory structure linking properties of elements and compounds to each other, and to their atomic structure. The reasoning involved in grasping Avogadro's hypothesis, and its appliation to formulae from volumes of reacting gases.

Can handle the conservation of elements in an exchange reaction, so for the first time has a model of chemical reaction. Use of balanced chemical equations is possible, provided that plenty of drill is given in learning the rules of the game. The relationship of chemical equations to reactions will be perceived, but do not expect pupils to know how to use them to estimate quantities except by practice in specified situations. May use atomic theory and simple model of atomic structure to account for chemical change.

The functional use of chemical symbols. The Nuffield approach to equations—from the experimental situation, through the nearest idealisation of the facts that fits the measurement, to a balanced equation. Mole concept usable deductively, and pupil can analyse problem to see how to apply translation into moles or molarities and translation back into volumes or masses. Equilibrium, as a dynamic process between reactants and products.

Reaction of acid with alkali is

$$H^+ + OH^- \rightarrow H_2O$$

Limits to change of pH by dilution alone. Acids are solutions; without water they are not acidic. Conservations during neutralisation: nothing lost, and new product in principle recoverable.
$N_1 V_1 = N_2 V_2$ problems, with practice.

The reaction between an acid and an alkali, understood in terms of the disturbance of the equilibrium between H^+ and OH^- ions in water. Use of molar quantities for finding equation of reaction between an acid and an alkali. Can appreciate that there are H^+ ions even in 1.0M sodium hydroxide, and hence has rational understanding of pH scale.

	Topic	2A *early concrete*	2B *late concrete*
C.7	Oxidation and Reduction	Pure oxygen makes things burn more brightly than air itself.	Carbon can reduce metal-oxides to metal. Oxygen can oxidise a metal. Metals can be placed in a reactivity series by their speed and vigour of burning.
C.8	Chemical Equilibria		Acids oppose alkalis—each will neutralise the other. Heat often breaks up chemicals. Chemicals often give off heat when they react. See C.2.
C.9	Chemicals and Energy	That one is stronger than this because it's hotter (or brighter).	You can compare them by seeing how much heat is given out, etc. An affinity for oxygen series. If you have to heat it, it must be a weak reaction. If you want more energy you either have to take an element at the top of the series, or take more.
C.10	Organic Chemistry		Names of simple compounds, and their physical properties.

3A early formal	*3B late formal*
Have a model of a chemical reaction, conserving the elements, so can predict that when carbon or a reactive metal reduces an oxide, carbon dioxide or a metal oxide must be produced. From a set of competition reactions can work out a reactivity series, and from a reactivity series can predict which reductions will succeed. Oxidation is increase of oxygen or other reactive non-metal.	Can appreciate that there are different theories or models of oxidation/reduction, and can critically compare them. Can use model of reaction even where what they *see* is paradoxical e.g. magnesium 'burning' in steam—gas produced *must* be hydrogen. Ready for a valency change or bond-forming account of oxidation.
A reaction may go further if you add excess of a chemical Not all reactions go all the way. Some reactions are reversible.	Can utilise a dynamic model of molecular or ionic collisions meaning that reaction is always going both ways (to some extent). Hence equilibrium in a 4-component system can be disturbed in both directions by adding excess on the opposite side. Can understand why *removing* a substance from one side can make equilibrium shift to that side.
Comparison of energies of reactions by measuring the heat given out (but from equimolar amounts only, if teacher sets it up that way). More energy evolved due to greater attraction of molecules or atoms.	You have to compare like with like, so equimolar quantities necessary. Use of energy level diagrams to answer questions. Comparison of the heats of reactions of chlorides with silver nitrate. Work and heat. Account in terms of molecular rearrangement in relation to kinetic energy of vibration. You can make (some) reactions run backwards by using electrical energy.
Classification of a few simple families in terms of their common functional group. Absence of the simpler 'rules' of ionic chemistry gives rise to confusion.	Reactions between compounds, and deductive/explanatory model of the properties of compounds in terms of their functional groups and 3D structure. Appreciates that there is a system of possible transformations between different families of compounds and can begin to store knowledge of system.

Approaches to biology

In addition to those given earlier in this chapter there is a further reason why it is difficult to apply this process of analysis to biological objectives. Although the *methods* of experimental design in biology are both easy to describe, and also sophisticated in their intellectual demand, the *concepts* are capable of some realisation at almost any cognitive level. This means that there is a complex web of inter-relationships between different topics at low, intermediate, and higher levels, and therefore many different starting-points and sequences which are possible, and many different ways of dividing the subject into areas of study. Should Nutrition be studied under Structure and Function or under Respiration? Ultimately what is wanted is some kind of map indicating to what depth pupils capable of 2A, 2B, 3A and then 3B thinking would find it possible to go in each of the major biological concepts. From this, feasible teaching sequences would follow naturally depending on the age and ability of the pupils under consideration. John

Table 9.3 *Biology*

Topic	2A *early concrete*	2B *late concrete*
B.1 Living things: Classification and Differentiation	Although it is possible to classify according to obvious properties, does not classify in terms of a hierarchy (class-inclusion). Thus difficulty found in classifying *birds* as animals. Details of animals and plants may be internalised, without understanding of the relationships between them. Thus simple observation and recording, the material of 'nature study', is available.	Begins to use rules of class-inclusion, but use of 'keys' is mystifying because it is a strategy based on the whole set of descriptors, and pupil is looking for the defining characteristics of each organism, e.g. insects have six legs.
B.2 Structure and Function	Structures and functions may be learned separately as discrete bits of information. A goat has big incisors and grinding molars. A goat eats grass. Even 'grass eating animals have grind-ing molars', as a bit of isolated information; but it is difficult to learn these bits of information because relationships are limited to one cause-one effect.	Either the organism has the given structure *because* of its lifestyle, or it has developed this lifestyle *because* it has this structure. Kestrels eat mice because their binocular vision lets them catch mice, or they have binocular vision because they like to eat mice. Cannot see both relationships operating at once.

Deadman [9] has provided such a description in the areas of genetics and evolution, derived from close observation and questioning of pupils. Here the modest aim has been attempted of providing a reasonable sample of objectives, classified under one set of arbitrary headings, to give the biology specialist some idea of what the map would be like by generalising from concrete instances. Provided an objective is clearly defined, its cognitive level of demand can be estimated by the methods of taxonomy 1 and 2 in the last chapter. Thus although *biology* cannot be defined and assessed in Table 9.3, many particular objectives *can*, and an approach is opened to the assessment of any one of the almost infinite number of biologies.

NOTE

1 'Any idea or problem or body of knowledge can be presented in a form simple enough so that any particular learner can understand it in a recognisable form'.[3]

3A *early formal*	3B *late formal*
Can construct and use 'keys' where field of decision-making is limited to a few organisms and obvious traits. Thus can use other people's systems of classification, provided their rules are explicit.	Can appreciate the problems involved in arriving at and using e.g. the linnean taxonomy. Now can give some meaning to the concept of a virus, because grasp of model of cell is sufficiently sophisticated.
In studying structure of, e.g. the kidney (Nuffield O-level Biology, Year IV) would be expected to grasp the salient features of the organ and its function i.e. use model that is given.	In studying kidney could be expected to model its functions and consider alternative hypotheses as to how the parts of the structure achieve their functions by checking the hypotheses against the evidence.

Topic	2A early concrete	2B late concrete
B.3 Growth	Growth as increase in size, as measured by height or weight. Growth not a constant phenomenon. Physical factors effect growth, e.g. poor nutrition.	Growth is the result of cellular division. Occurs in special areas in plants. In humans some parts grow faster than others. For humans, appreciation that different measurements of growth are not necessarily related to one another, e.g. height and weight.
B.4 Respiration, Nutrition and Transport	Food gives energy. Heart as a pump (from experience of own pulse). Blood flows to parts of body and to lungs delivering and collecting.	Respiration provides air (oxygen) so food can be used/broken down to give energy. The heart and lungs are a circulation system to facilitate this. Transport of food in plants: experiment of ringing, cutting phloem vessels, and so simple associative relation between phloem and transport.
B.5 Reproduction (Note that in its personal implications for each pupil this will be an emotive topic. Cognitive stage is probably less important than stage of psycho-sexual development).	Reproduction necessary for increasing numbers and for perpetuating the species i.e. knows what would happen if no cats had kittens.	Reproduction leads to the continuous replacement of each type of organism. Differences between sexual and asexual reproduction, as a learned set of criteria. Simple cause-effect action of hormones, e.g. puberty. In sexual reproduction, two 'special' cells combine to form embryo. The mechanism of fertilisation in plants and animals.
B6 Ecosystem	See B.1.	Simple cause-effect relationships in ethology. Population dynamics in the sense: lots of aphids—later lots of ladybirds. Simple food chains.

3A early formal	*3B late formal*
Different measures of growth not necessarily related, for other organisms, e.g. height/weight of plant in dark. Simultaneous processes of cellular enlargement and specialisation in animals and plants. Growth rates.	Process of nuclear division and energy transformations, multiple interactions of factors effecting growth. Cell-division in eggs as sequenced by genetic code for differentiation of organs.
Gas transport in plants. Diffusion appreciated analytically: simultaneous O_2/CO_2 movement across membranes in lungs, etc. Efficiency of capillaries in distribution to cells. Pressure as force per unit area, and valve function in terms of pressure differentials. Transpiration pull in terms of evaporation causing water to be pulled up. Functional relationship between capillaries, cells, lymph and diffusion. Osmosis as a process occurring between solutions of different strengths.	Homeostasis. Plasmolysis and turgidity. Extension of model of semi-permeable membrane to root hair and osmotic unit. The need for transport systems in terms of the ratio of volume to surface area of body. Model of osmosis as differential vapour pressure or 'activity' of solvent.
There are equal numbers of chromosomes in body cells after division, hence chromosomes must be split. Offspring must have same number of chromosomes as each parent so gametes must have half as many chromosomes as other cells. Every cell in the body has the same chromosomes in the nucleus.	Perceives the advantages of sexual reproduction in allowing for variation, and so for changes in the species with time. The functions of meiosis and mitosis.
Relationship of an organ to its organism, and an organism to its habitat. Biomass, in relation to food chains, graphically represented. The Nitrogen cycle. The Carbon cycle.	The subtleties of ecological balance. Multiple equilibria in the environment, and the difficulty (impossibility?) of predicting the outcomes of changes in one factor. Relative effects of competition, and understanding of dynamic mechanism of succession.

	Topic	2A *early concrete*	2B *late concrete*
B.7	Evolution and Genetics		See B.1 and B.2
B.8	Chemical Processes		See C.5, 6, 7, and 8. See C.3 for interpretation of speeds of reaction at 2B, 3A, and 3B.
B.9	Experimental Design	To see if something, e.g. fertiliser, produces an effect, will try it, with no attempt to provide a comparison except in a before and after sense.	Will see the necessity for a comparison and will probably be satisfied by a 'one with and one without' design. Ignores other variables when testing for each.
B.10	Control and Coordination	Simple connections, e.g. 'We sweat when we are hot'.	Simple reflex and learned responses. Much descriptive physiology of the sense organs, structure of the skin, etc. but no interrelations. Hormones as chemical messengers.

3A early formal	*3B late formal*
May tolerate both directions of cause-effect-cause operating at once, or even multi-cause/multi-effect, but sees the process as a series of small steps, not integrated as a continuous process. Can use a given model of natural selection as a post hoc explanation of certain structures: deer's acute sense of hearing allows it to survive, and so breed, etc.	Can operate with the concept of a whole organism developing in a particular environment, with each part of its structure harmonising with function imposed by its environment. Would be able to discuss advantages and disadvantages of specialisation of structure to environment.
Can be expected to interpret 'oxidation' as a substance-breaking and energy-releasing process (provided some experience of chemistry is also taught). Can readily interpret reactions of carbon dioxide as a weak acid, but structural formulae of carbo-hydrate products of photosynthesis are too complex a model to which to attach any chemical meaning. But the process of photosynthesis would be understood as energy storage (larger molecules). At this level 'Heat' and 'Temperature' are clearly differentiated, and calorific values interpreted. But the principle of most chemical tests would not be understood.	This level is required for even a minimal understanding of the chemical significance of the molecules present in food and digestive products (backed up by a sixth form knowledge of Chemistry—see C.10) Understanding of how a 'buffer' works.
Can produce a strategy of control experiments in relation to obvious variables which may interfere, but often fail to see the importance of the experiment in which a possible factor is *not* present, and may fail to eliminate the effect of interfering variables in interpreting the results unless they have model of how they contribute.	Provision of controls and the use of these in interpreting results are integrated by their grasp of the possible combinations of variables in the system as a whole. May appreciate that variables may interact. Begins to see that sampling is essential if natural variation is to be 'controlled'.
Understands that action-reaction is insufficient to explain complex behaviour. Principle of feedback applied to hormonal and nervous systems, as a circular causal chain, rather than as an equilibrium.	Homeostasis. The maintenance of a steady state by feedback systems in dynamic equilibrium. Relationship of individual systems to the whole organism.

10 Testing of the CAT— and so testing Piaget

If the CAT is to meet the use prescribed for it, as a tool which can be used by any science teacher, it must be shown that it is *reliable*, and that it is *valid*. In this context, reliability can be demonstrated by the measure of agreement between different individuals who use the CAT to assess the cognitive demand levels of the same set of objectives. An important measure of validity will be the extent to which these assessments made by teachers do accurately predict the success or failure at the objectives of pupils whose cognitive stages have been estimated. Such a validity-check, if successful, will add significantly to the weight of evidence supporting the Piagetian model on which the CAT is founded. The questions of both reliability and validity of the CAT have been investigated, and it is now possible to give some answers in quantitative terms.

Agreement trial for the use of CAT

During the development of the taxonomies, a consultative committee was formed of experienced science teachers from comprehensive and grammar schools, and of other science educators. This committee met on three occasions at four-month intervals to discuss in detail their use of successive drafts of the taxonomies on particular lessons taken from well-known Teachers' Guides. With their help the process of curriculum-analysis was developed from a personal skill to one in which the criteria of judgement were spelled out and held in common. The process had become more objective. Nevertheless the possibility remained that the group had criteria which were used in the same way, but which had escaped being written

Table 10.1 Examples of objectives and test items to be used in testing CAT.

Topic		Objective		Exam items testing objective	Cognitive level of objective
(3) *NP–I.13 p. 35–37 Different heavinesses	A	'To carry out the experiment on the $3 \times 4 \times 5$ blocks only and to put the blocks in order of increasing heaviness. To interpret the results as telling them that iron is a heavier kind of metal than aluminium.'	6.	Suppose you had a hollow dart. Which of the 6 materials would you put inside it to make it as heavy as possible?	2A
(20) *NC A1.1 p. 16–19 Pure salt from rock-salt	A	'To carry out the experiment and to realise that the end product after evaporation of water is purified salt.'	42	What is the white product produced? Which is purer, the rock-salt or the white powder?	2A
	B	'To interpret the results in terms of the reversible process of salt dissolving in water, which can be recovered by boiling off the water.'	42	What things were in the liquid which passed through the filter-paper? Explain what happens in the three steps so as to make this a process of purification.	2B
(30) *NCS7-2a p. 93–96 also 2c p. 97–99	A	'To find, as a result of the experiments, that yeast breaks down sugars to a gas which is called carbon dioxide.'	63	What two things were producing the gas? What was the gas?	2B
Yeast action	B	'To appreciate the purpose of *each* of the experiments and to deduce the effects validly of temperature, sugar, and yeasts.'	64	Which flasks would you compare to tell the effect of temperature? Which flasks would you need in order to prove that *yeast* is needed to make the gas?	3A

*NP = Nuffield O level Physics: Guide to experiments I
NC = Nuffield O level Chemistry: The Sample Scheme, Stages I & II: The Basic Course
NCS = Nuffield Combined Science, Teachers Guide II

down and thus made public. When an agreement trial was planned it was necessary not only to compare this trained group with each other when each assessed curriculum objectives independently, but also to compare the group's agreement consistency with that of a fresh sample of assessors who had access only to the written materials printed in this book (Chapter 8, with the assistance of some of the Chapter 3 material and a shorter version of Chapter 9). To the original group of ten committee members were added fifteen experienced science teachers who had expressed an interest in the process of curriculum analysis.

For the trial, a set of objectives was prepared from thirty topics distributed among physics, chemistry, and biology commonly taught in the first three years of secondary education. The level of thinking demanded by the objectives was hypothesised to require a range from early concrete to late formal operational. Thus the ability of the taxonomy to produce consistent assessments in the hands of experienced science teachers would be tested at all levels. In many cases two or three objectives would be defined for each topic to shed light on a common problem: that of presenting a topic at different depths of treatment to suit a particular class of pupils. Examples of these objectives are given in Table 10.1, with their assumed level of thinking required. Sample test items are added, to help in defining the objectives more closely.

Table 10.2 Distribution of objectives by subject and by levels.

Level	Physics	Chemistry	Biology	Number at each level planned	Number at each level assessed (mean)
3B	5	3	4	12	12
3A	9	7	4	20	21
2B	8	6	7	21	18
2A	6	3	2	11	13
Totals	28	19	17	64	64

A total of 64 objectives were prepared in this way, and Table 10.2 shows how they were selected according to level and subject area, to achieve the intended distribution. (The figures in the last column indicate the number of objectives the panel estimated to be at each level.)

For each of these 64 objectives, the assessors were asked both to produce an overall assessment of each objective, and to list which of the categories, at which level, in the CAT they had used in arriving at their judgements. In this way the categories themselves could be compared with each other for any systematic differences and for any deficiencies in the behavioural descriptions in each cell of the taxonomy.

In the end seven of the consultative committee and nine of newcomers managed to complete the very demanding exercise of assessing all the objectives, and of recording all of the categories they had used. With the two members of the CSMS team, this gave a group of eighteen in all.

Degree of agreement on levels of objectives

It was found that 13 of the 64 Objectives were ambiguous in spite of the effort made to avoid this source of variation. This was found both from personal comments made by the assessors, and statistically[1]. For purposes of correlational analysis these 13 objectives were eliminated, and the degree of agreement was calculated on the 51 objectives which remained. As a measure of reliability the mean individual correlation between each person's judgement, and that of the mean of all the assessors was 0.84. The mean standard deviation between the judgements on each objective by all assessors was 1.0, on an equal interval scale ranging from 1 = pre-operational, through early concrete = 2, late concrete = 4, to late formal = 8.

The meaning of these figures in terms of practical decisions is that one person's assessment of one objective estimates confidently the true level of the objective only as closely as ±2 intervals around the assessment he/she has made. But two-thirds of the time the estimate will be within ±1 intervals from the true value. If a person assesses an objective at the early formal level (3A), there is a 5 per cent chance that the true mean may be as low as 2B or as high as 3B, but it probably lies between 2B/3A and 3A/3B. For many purposes relating to everyday decisions about the choice of curriculum activities this precision may be close enough. But if, for example, a group of teachers is working together on new curriculum materials and needs to estimate more precisely the levels of various objectives being considered, the estimation error can be reduced by using more than one assessor. If four people independently assess the objective then the limits within which the true mean is likely to differ from the mean of their estimates will be reduced to ±1 interval. Four heads are twice as good as one[2]. This is the precision which can realistically be expected from people using the taxonomies for the first time, and without a background of the work of Piaget.

The categories as sources of judgement

At the same time as the assessments produced by different assessors were compared, it was also possible to find out whether any of the categories were yielding assessments which were incompatible with the other categories. This will be discussed in more detail shortly when the consistency of Piaget's theory is mentioned, but here it can be said that none of the categories showed serious systematic error in relation to the others. But as a result of comments made, and of noting cases where more than one level of assessment was made for a given objective using a category, it was possible to clarify distinctions between the descriptions in one cell and the next, and to add behavioural descriptions where it was found that one cell in the draft CAT (for example the 2B cell for 1.4, Use of Models) was being used seldom or never by assessors.

Consultative committee v. newcomers

One of the purposes of the research was to test whether the CAT, together with its introductory comment and training exercises, contained sufficient information to allow an intelligent and perseverant newcomer to analyse the cognitive demand of science curricula. A preliminary analysis of the data gave little support to the idea that the consultative committee were using criteria which remained tacit. The performance of the three groups is compared in Figure 10.1. The upper set of points joined by solid lines show the correlations between the mean of everyone's judgements and the judgements of each individual assessor. This gives a measure of how well the assessors agree with each other, and so of the reliability of the CAT. (The sub-set of 51 non-ambiguous objectives was used in computing these values; values for the whole set of 64 are about 0.05 lower.)

It can be seen that the newcomers assessments were little different in reliability from those of the consultative committee. Even the rather low value of person 15 was due largely to an unwillingness ever to use the 3B level, rather than unreliability of judgement. We will see that this person's assessments agree better with reality than they do with those of other assessors.

Since the newcomers had access only to written materials such as are present in this book, it can be concluded that the goal of providing for

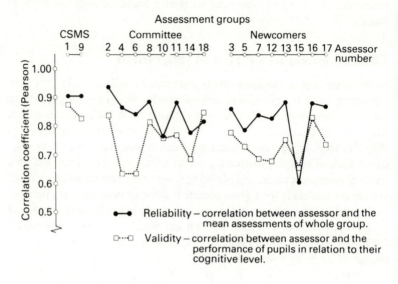

Figure 10.1 Reliability and validity of persons assessing 64 science objectives.

teachers who have little or no acquaintance with Piaget's work the means of correctly assessing the levels of thinking demanded by science lessons has been achieved. But it would be as unwise to conclude from this that a period of training, for the average science teacher, would not be helpful, as to conclude that if one has a good text-book no teacher is needed. This group of experienced teachers must have been unusually self-motivated to complete an assignment like this, most of them in term-time, and all on their own, since independence of working was one of the conditions of the research. The learning of the expertise of curriculum-analysis would best be done by talking-out between a group of colleagues, or as a form of inservice training.

The reality-test: how well does the CAT predict pupils' understanding and what does this say about Piaget's theory?

In Chapter 6 we described how the stages of cognitive development of pupils in groups were estimated using Science Reasoning Tasks, how these pupils were then taught sections of Nuffield Combined Science, and finally tested to check whether predictions made on the basis of pupil estimates and curriculum assessments were verified. The method used to check the validity of the CAT was essentially similar to this, the critical difference being that on this occasion the assessments of demand level of curriculum objectives were made, not by one or two specialists, but by science teachers using the CAT as given in Chapter 8.

We noted above that the 64 objectives prepared for the CAT trials were chosen so that they could be tested on pupils in schools. This was ensured by using lesson material from either the Nuffield Combined Science course, or the first two years of the Nuffield O level courses. For the purposes of this research, objectives were grouped according to the Section of Nuffield Combined Science in which they occurred, or in the year of the O level course concerned. A structured-question type of examination, as used in Nuffield O level exams to test understanding rather than rote-learning was prepared for each group of objectives. In this technique of examining, pupils are reminded (often by diagrams) of work they have done or apparatus they have used. They are provided with data, and then given many questions which test their ability to handle the data according to the concepts which are the course objectives. Schools were approached in which the pupils had recently completed such sections of work, and the teachers were asked both to administer the short examination of the course content and also to give their pupils one of the SRTs described in Chapter 4 to serve as an estimate of the present cognitive level of each of the pupils. For each section at least two school classes were used, usually in different schools, in an attempt to control for different kinds of teaching.

The exam items were marked on a simple right or wrong basis, and had been written with this mode of assessment in mind. For each objective the items relating to it were either grouped according to a two-thirds success principle similar to that used in the SRTs (if a pupil got two-thirds of the items right, he was said to have understood the objective) or they were assessed individually by the following method. The pupils were grouped according to the level (2A, 2B, 2B/3A, etc) at which they had performed on the SRT. For each item the percentage of the pupils estimated at the 2A level who passed the item were calculated, followed by the percentage of those at the 2A/2B level who passed, and so on. From the graph of these values the level of the item (and hence the objective) was judged by interpolation—the level at which 67 per cent of the pupils were successful. For the purposes of making a numerical scale, 2A was numbered 2, 2B 4, 3A 6, and 3B 8. In this way each objective was given a number estimating its level of cognitive demand on a continuous scale. This is shown in Figure 10.2 with respect to objective 43, for which there were two items. Although the

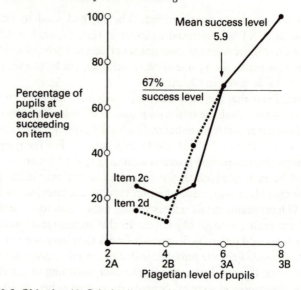

Fig. 10.2 Objective 43: Solution/evaporation model of purification of rock-salt.

assessors were asked to assess each objective as either 2A, 2B, 3A, or 3B (with 2B/3A as the only intermediate suggested), the mean of all eighteen assessors was also expressed as a number on a continuous scale from 2 to 8. In this way their assessment of the objectives could be used as a prediction of the cognitive level required in a pupil for understanding of the objective's content.

In all, seven examinations were written and fifteen schools provided classes, some more than one. Between 50 and 120 pupils provided data relating to each of the objectives. At the time of writing this research is incomplete, having covered 40 of the objectives, but information on 56 will be published in specialist journals when schools have been found in which they have been taught.

In Figure 10.1 (p. 110), the crosses joined by a broken line show how the assessment made by each individual correlates with the actual level of each objective, as indicated by the levels of the pupils who achieved the objectives. This is one measure of the validity of the CAT—a measure of how well assessments made with the CAT agree with reality. Given the extra element of error involved in the estimation of pupils' stages, this may be considered quite satisfactory.

When one looks at the mean value of all the assessments made, and compares them with the 'real' value, the picture that emerges is one of

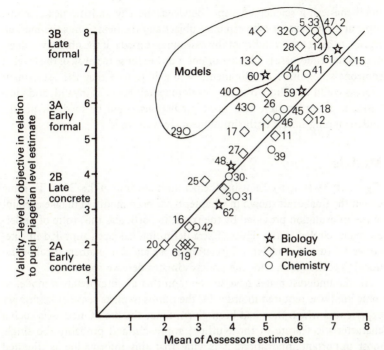

Fig. 10.3 Validity trial of CAT: Prediction of cognitive level of science objectives.

generally consistent and accurate prediction. In Figure 10.3, the means of assessors' CAT estimates of objectives on the 2A–3B scale of 1 to 8 is plotted against the levels of objectives as revealed by pupil performance. The closeness of each objective to the diagonal line is a measure of the accuracy of prediction. There is a group of points, enclosed in Figure 10.3 with the label 'models', which represent objectives for which the CAT assessments were underestimates of the 'real' level of the objectives. These are worthy of more detailed discussion below.

Overall, however, it can be seen that the level of agreement is sufficient to validate the curriculum taxonomy, and so also the Piagetian theory that lies behind it. As with the work described in Chapters 6 and 7, the level of success of predictions made here is powerful evidence in support of the Piagetian model of stages of development on which they are based. The acid test of Piaget's theory is whether a pupil is sufficiently consistent in the strategies of thinking he uses for predictions to be made. Even if the assessments made with the help of the CAT were perfectly valid, they would be useless if nothing consistent could be said about the likelihood of a given pupil mastering science concepts between one day and the next, or one topic and the next, or between one subject and the next. Thus the method chosen to assess the validity of the assessments made of the objectives does, at the same time, assess whether or not it makes sense to speak of the level of someone's cognitive development. While it is true that the assessment process could be valid while the developmental theory is invalid, and vice-versa, it is not possible that good predictions could be made of pupils' understanding unless both simultaneously were valid.

Models

Figure 10.3 was arrived at using the penultimate draft of the CAT. To some extent the final draft shown in Chapter 8 has been modified to take account of the information provided by the trials, in particular the group of under-estimates circled in the figure. Extra definition has been supplied in categories 1.4 (use of models), 1.3 (relationships), and 2.4 (mathematical operations). Yet the reasons for the underestimates deserve comment.

All the underestimates have in common that an interpretative model of some kind was required in order for the pupils to make sense of laboratory experiences which they had been given. Since the use of models is such a characteristic feature of the Nuffield approach, and probably the single most important innovation, it is vital that this information is digested by science teachers planning to use the approach on younger or less able pupils. Perhaps the most surprising example is objective 29, which was:

> To recognise that chromatography separates the different coloured substances in grass/leaves.

In this experiment, grass is ground in a mortar together with sand and a little acetone, and then chromatographed from the centre of a filter paper with drops of fresh acetone. Pupil after pupil, attempting to apply the strategies of concrete operational thinking, attributed the yellow to the sand and the green to the grass. They were simply classifying the different materials according to their major characteristic. Only those pupils who on other items showed that they could use the model of a 'pure substance' were prepared to interpret what was before their eyes as the separation of *two* pure substances from each other, both having come from the grass. Objective 28 involved explaining the 'spongy' behavior of steam in terms of a simple kinetic model, and objective 40 required a reversible model of water as a hydrogen/oxygen compound. In objective 13, which in relation to the experiments bearing on Floating and Sinking was:

To carry out the experiments with various blocks and newtonmeters, and to realise that a loss in pull of the blocks suspended in water is accompanied by the same increase in the downward push of the beaker of water.   (36, section 6.2e)

Only the pupils having the capacity for late formal (3B) thinking made any sense in their replies to test items bearing on the problem. In the test the pupils were given a table with typical results such as they might have obtained themselves. No-one *could* make sense of such results without an active interpretative model, and it can be seen (1.4–3B) that in this case they must also be able to make quantitative deductions from the model.

Objectives 4 and 5 involve calculating the density of air after it has been 'weighed' by removing a number of litre-boxfulls from an inflated plastic cubical container, and then calculating the weight of air in the laboratory. Objectives 32 and 33 involved calculating the density of oxygen from various gas syringe experiments, objective 14 embodied the Archimedes principle, and objective 60 involved estimating the water-loss of a whole tree per day, given information on the loss from the leaves of one branch, and the number of leaves on branch and tree. With this latter group the modelling involved was *mathematical* modelling. Just as someone learning to use a microscope on tissues gradually learns by thought and experience to *see* cells and structures in what was initially an uninterpretable jumble, so too until the pupil can see the whole set of additive and ratio-type operations which link the observations he has made, he will find only confusion and be unable to impose meaning by his calculations. Note particularly that we are *not* asserting that there is high cognitive demand in the individual computations involved in these experiments. It is the ability to model the situation in terms of a set of linked mathematical relationships, prior to computation, that we are attempting to describe.

NOTES

1 The mean of the standard deviations of judgements made for this group of objectives differed from the mean of the standard deviations of the other 51 objectives by eight standard errors. Thus this group had systematic sources of variation over and above the random variation among assessors.

2 Statistically, 95 per cent confidence limits for the estimation of a mean from a sample are between ±2 standard deviations of the population divided by the square root of the number in the sample.

Part 4

11 The match

The time has come to draw together the two main sets of evidence presented in this book, and to see what their implications are for science teaching and curriculum development. We now have:

(a) a well developed method of assessing levels of cognitive development of groups of pupils, and the comprehensive data on the British school population collected by this method;

(b) a validated method of analysing science curricula to establish the levels of cognitive demand that they make.

In this chapter we will discuss the match of some modern science curricula to their target populations, and consider the empirical curriculum development process which gave rise to such examples of mismatch.

Nuffield Combined Science (NCS) has featured rather prominently in the preceding chapters. It is an important case since it is by far the most popular of the published curricula in use in England and Wales with the 11–13 age range, and it typifies much of what came to be known as the 'Nuffield approach' during the 70s. While such an all-embracing label may no longer be appropriate for all of the material which carries the Nuffield imprimateur, the approach remains a significant force in science education on both sides of the Atlantic.

Combined Science was derived originally from the first two or three years of the separate Nuffield O level biology, chemistry, and physics courses. These had been designed for a selective school population (the top 20 per cent) but the NCS team aimed to broaden the ability range for which their course would be suitable, and in the introduction it is described as appropriate for 'average pupils'. The evidence presented in Chapters 6 and 10 suggests that this aim has not been attained. An average first form, if such a group existed, would contain no more than 11 per cent of pupils capable of even early formal operational thinking. Analysis of any of the units of NCS will reveal a number of activities requiring early formal, and some which need late formal thinking, in the first year.

But the problem is more serious than this. In all of the units we have looked at closely (notably Sections 4, 6, 7, and 8) it is not simply that *some* activities are beyond the reach of most of the pupils, but that it is these high level objectives which are the key to the whole unit. If they are not grasped, then there is little point in the pupil doing the unit at all. We have likened this to the process of leading children half way up a cliff, from the top of which interesting territory could be explored—if the top were ever reached [55].

Notable examples include the investigation of floating in Section 6, and the development of pressure concepts in Section 4. Analysis of the density concept, and subsequent experimental confirmation, shows that early formal operations are required to make any interpretation of the question 'why do some objects float?'. If pupils cannot reach the conclusion that an object will float if its weight is less than that of the water it displaces, then all of the experiments and speculation will achieve only mystification. The key to the pressure problem is the comprehension of pressure as force per unit area, which involves the ratio of two independent variables and so demands early formal operational thinking. If, as is most likely, these concepts are introduced in years 1 or 2 (grades 6 or 7) we submit that 80 per cent of pupils will be mystified.

A more subtle example of mismatch is revealed in Section 8. We found (Chapter 6) that the performance of pupils on a test of objectives (whose individual demand levels had been analysed) was lower than would be expected from estimates made of the pupils' cognitive levels. This was true especially for the chemical topics, where 3A pupils achieved an average facility of only 35 per cent on 3A items, and 2B pupils an average of 31 per cent on 2B items. One likely explanation for this is that the section as a whole makes demands over and above those made by its constituent activities. It seems as if the authors of this section had sensed the inherent difficulty of many of the linking concepts in chemistry (see Chapter 9) and so presented each of the activities in an empirical way, often making no more than concrete demands. But as such they appear to the pupil as a series of individual activities which bear no relation to one another. The connecting range of peaks, which provide the model necessary to an interpretation of the experiences, is missed.

This worthy attempt to temper the concepts to the (shorn) lamb thus fails for a more obscure reason. The assumption that empirical descriptions are easier than those ordered or interpreted by a model is a fallacy. The object of a model is to reduce the cognitive load, not to increase it. Concrete thinking is not stored amorphous fact, but facts structured according to definite rules.

We must admit at this point that we have used Combined Science as something of a whipping boy, to stand for its older brothers the Nuffield O level courses since it does conveniently illustrate many of the conceptual difficulties of those courses. But we retain a great deal of respect for these courses. The 'Nuffield approach' includes the key ideas of *guided discovery*, and of *integrating concepts*. Through a selected and structured series of practical investigations the pupil is led to discover something of the way that things behave. Patterns such as the periodic table, the relation of form to function, and the kinetic theory perform an essential integrating function which not only makes the atomic discoveries meaningful and memorable, but also allows for interpolation and extrapolation from what has been discovered to what has not.

Behind this approach lies the implicit conviction that unless the pupil sees for himself the way in which the concept puts a useful construction on the events which it co-relates, he has not really grasped the concept. He may get the right words, but would not have the means of applying them. The Nuffield O level and CS materials assume that the pupil can perceive for himself the connections between the practical discoveries and the concepts but that unless he has had the experience, he cannot create or use the concept. We are adding only that if the pupil does not have the inner capacity yet to make the connections, he will fail to understand the concept even if he is given the experimental experiences. For those who do have the capacity, the courses are brilliant examples of stimulating material.

Our comments on the O level courses and NCS should not be taken to extend to all science curricula developed under the Nuffield umbrella. For instance, a sharp contrast is provided by *Nuffield Secondary Science* (NSS). This is a set of materials for teachers, with some worksheets for pupils. It was never designed as a course, to be followed in a particular sequence, but rather as a 'mine' of material from which teachers could quarry nuggets to suit their own course needs. NSS was designed for pupils in years 3 to 5 (grades 8–10) of the secondary modern schools—the schools to which three-quarters of the population went when the 11+ examination was used to select the top 15–20 per cent to go to grammar schools. In the context of a comprehensive school, NSS material would be intended for those pupils who are not taking O level examinations, but who might follow CSE or

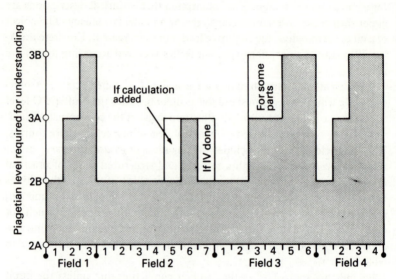

Fig. 11.1 Level of thinking required by different topics in NSS 'Harnessing Energy'.

non-examination courses. The great majority of such children leave school at 16 years.

Since NSS is not a course, one cannot plot a diagram of cognitive demand year by year, as can be done with the other curricula discussed. But a detailed look at the ideas and experiences proposed in NSS reveal a well-graduated series of routines, initially well within the reach of concrete operational thinking, as shown in Figure 11.1. In principle it would be possible to select from NSS materials suitable for any class, or to allow different pupils to study each field to a different depth. Thus in terms of meeting the needs of the average pupil, NSS is more successful than NCS. This should not be surprising when one remembers that the latter originated in the empirical experiences of selective school teachers, whereas the former was made by teachers whose experience was in secondary modern schools.

Recent developments

The era of the massive, headquarters-orientated, science curriculum project has passed for the time being, and the most recent new material that is being published is generally the result of some modifications of, or drawing-upon existing material. It is often developed locally through small scale projects involving perhaps one or two local education authorities. This is not just a result of a shortage of money, but also of a recognition of the different needs of different localities. Local curriculum projects bring with them also the benefits in teacher education of involving many trial schools and of the sort of personal supervision that is only possible in a limited geographical area. Possibly this trend also reflects some impatience on the part of the major funding bodies with the science educators' apparently insatiable craving for new curriculum projects.

From the core of Nuffield Combined Science has grown the *Themes for the Middle Years*. This consists of a series of beautifully designed work cards and study cards for pupils and notes for teachers which are intended to extend the range of Combined Science downwards in both years and ability. The way in which this aim has been attempted, though, resembles that of the chemistry mentioned on p. 120, and may produce the same snags. In the Water theme, for example, while the newtonmeters of NCS have been removed from the floating/sinking problem, the intention is still that the pupils should relate the density of the object to the density of the liquid by intelligent experimentation, and the conceptual demand level described in Chapter 3 remains.

Nuffield 13 to 16 is a set of modules for teachers which has grown partly from *Nuffield Secondary Science*, but it draws also on the *Schools Council Integrated Science Project*, a high demand O level curriculum which includes a significant measure of social concern in its science. Since *13 to 16* builds on a core-plus-enrichment-activities principle within the units, and grades each activity with one, two, or three stars according to estimated difficulty, it shares with NSS and ASEP (see p. 32) the possibility of providing materials for pupils at each stage. It remains to be seen what variety of courses teachers are able to create using this source.

The evidence and line of reasoning presented in this book were not available to the developers of the original Nuffield material, and had only just started to appear in the academic journals when the revised O level courses, *Themes*, and *13 to 16* were in preparation. Although the evidence of mismatch was considered then to be controversial, some note was taken of it, and some attempts made to accommodate the new material to the findings of CSMS. A good example is the revision of the mole concept work in Nuffield O level chemistry, by moving it later in the course, and providing nomograms to eliminate the mass-mole conversion calculations. While this in itself does not lower the cognitive demand level of the mole concept, it does mean that pupils with only a hazy notion of moles can complete the practical work and obtain results. Deferring the full use of the mole by eighteen months to year five should fit the developmental pattern of more pupils.

So, some note was taken of cognitive matching problems by the curricula of the late 70s, but none took the limits imposed by the developmental level of children in British schools, first published in 1976 [51], as a major constraint on the design of their courses. This is understandable enough given the time it takes for an idea, however well supported, to become acceptable to the educational establishment. It is one of the purposes of this book to ensure that no science curriculum development of the future can proceed without at least having a method available for matching the demand level of the proposed material to the target population.

It can be seen that the approach presented in this book is not intended as a critique of the 'Nuffield approach'. It is in fact integral with it, and with the implied assumption of many modern maths courses which is that an ability to produce the right calculation response given to a contextual stimulus is of very limited value. Indeed, we wish to use the *same* approach in our suggestions for the immense work of invention which lies ahead. But the manner in which this principle will be realised would be quite different when concrete operations only are utilised. Both science and mathematics consist of conceptual systems. In the case of science they are more bound up with the concrete particulars of the subject of study; with mathematics the self-consistency of the language matters more. But in both studies it is the ability of the child to move within the system that is of value. It is this that he will take away with him when he has forgotten how to do his exam questions. We are merely trying to produce an explanation for a fact that has been amply confirmed, both in Britain and the United States by the empirical experience of teachers, that the first crop of 'new' science courses grossly overestimated the ability of children to handle new learning experiences.

The ideals of the Nuffield approach, however sympathetic we may be to them as ideals, can now be recognised as having led to a signficant *rise* in the level of cognitive demand of science courses. The basic structure of concepts which knit together the traditional O level courses from the third, or early in the fourth year have a quality of description similar to the behaviours recorded in *The Growth of Logical Thinking* as being early formal. This can also be seen from the descriptive analysis presented in Chapter 9. But the Piagetian level required for sixth form science, and for the Nuffield O level courses, is late formal.

One may well ask how this raising of the cognitive demand levels occurred, at the very time that terms such as 'curriculum evaluation', 'feedback', and 'school trials' had come into common usage amongst educators. Curriculum developers of the 60s and early 70s seemed to have an intuitive understanding of what makes scientific investigation different from other kinds of activity, but at the time no model was available to describe the likelihood of children of different ages and abilities understanding such material. Inevitably they had to use the experience of the children they had taught, and memory of their own development. We now know that the top 15 per cent of pupils develops cognitively at a much higher rate as compared with the average than had been realised, and the top 5 per cent are a similar way ahead of those 15 per cent from the top. As a result, the scant regard that the Nuffield O level teams paid to sampling—even sampling of the grammar school population that was their target—turned out to have far more serious consequences than they could reasonably have expected.

The evolution of the specialist science subject course, so similar in all countries in Europe and many in the Third World, does not inevitably follow from the nature of science itself. It has followed instead from the pattern of cognitive development of the small proportion of the population (perhaps only the top 10 per cent) who, in the last sixty years, have had access to secondary education. The teachers have adapted to the pupils they taught. The further the pupils could be 'got on', the further they were taken towards the practice of university science. That there is no end to the slippery slope of distortion of what is desirable educationally is shown by the evolution of the Nuffield O level courses. These ended up attuned, in terms of age, to the developmental pattern of an even smaller number of pupils: the top 5 per cent. We have noted before that if you are looking for the 'best' teachers to use their experience, practise, and ideas to develop new curricula, you are most likely to find them in the 'best' schools teaching the 'best' children. The rest of the story writes itself.

Does the same picture apply in the humanities?

At this point, one may well ask whether a similar process has taken place in the humanities. Is it only science and mathematics which make such heavy intellectual demands that the cognitive development of the pupils is a significant factor?

It seems very probable—although the evidence is thin on the ground—that the problem is more acute in science and mathematics. Research on evidence provided by GCE examination boards [41] has shown that the same examinees achieve significantly lower grades on O level science subjects than in many from the arts and that students matched on ability achieve higher grades on A level arts subjects, suggesting that the intellectual demands of the science subjects are higher. This can be interpreted in terms of what has in the past been (though no longer) social pressure from the universities who, faced with more students applying than there were places for, put up the standards for entry. Competitive schools would obviously raise the standard of their science teaching, and thus the pass criteria of the examination boards would rise, and school work would more and more resemble early university work. Yet research both in the teaching of history and in the comprehension of literature and geography has successfully used a developmental model to interpret students performance. In Taxonomy 1.6 (p. 74) the work of Peel and his students [42] at Birmingham on English and geography was used as a source of the descriptions with the intention of covering passages requiring different levels of comprehension (in particular in biology). But there is reason to believe that the competitive effect which makes itself felt through the public examination system has had a smaller distorting force in these subjects. In history, Hallam [15] has shown that O level teaching makes no demands higher than that of concrete operational thinking, and that formal thinking is brought in only for students who in sixth forms are in the run-up to university entrance, when it becomes part of their organisational style in essays which they begin to write to reinterpret what hitherto has been mainly factual. They now have to begin to look for underlying causes which can readily be seen (taxonomy 1.1; 1.2) to be an early formal characteristic. It seems as though, by empirical means, the teachers of history have adapted to the rather wider range of students who traditionally have studied their subject to O level and beyond.

No such close analyses of examination style have been studied in the other humanities subjects as yet, so that it is not possible to say to what extent in geography, say, intellectual specialisation has taken place in Britain. We look forward, then, with great interest to a by-product of the validation research reported in Chapter 7. In 1979 about 600 third-year (13[+]) selective and comprehensive school pupils were given five different Piagetian SRTs as a severe test of the consistency of the Piagetian developmental model. Eighteen months later, in June 1980 these pupils were sitting GCE and CSE examinations. They were probably the most precisely estimated sample (in Piagetian terms) ever to be investigated, and the detailed performance on all the external exam subjects will give valuable evidence on the extent to which cognitive development is a limiting factor in each school subject.

Some assumptions of High Science teaching

Both authors have in the past identified themselves first with the concept/
experience integrating paradigm of the 60s, and then with the belief that
this approach is so valuable for stimulating understanding in pupils that it
was obvious to look for ways of adapting it for the average pupil. We
believed that we could retain the method, and the games or routines that go
with it, since it was seen as a 'non-academic' approach which would not
alienate such children. Now we are propounding the view that as the profession of science teachers has faced the new problem of science for all, the
curriculum-modification process by which it has worked is all wrong. Some
explanation seems in order for such a change of mind.

Any science teacher, whether biologist, chemist, or physicist, experiences
during his training a process of identification with his or her specialist
subject. Such a process of commitment does have some aspect of faith—'a
willing suspension of disbelief'—that the discipline is of value, in its own
right. Although it is also a matter of faith that everything within the science
is capable of independent verification, in practice one trusts that the
community of established scientists has already done much of this. Our
approach to curriculum practice was shaken initially by the experience of
working with pupils according to our assumptions. It was they who told us,
or told the teachers using our curricula, that they couldn't understand, and
didn't care for the 'stimulating' fare that we were placing before them. But
to proceed from this to acceptance that *what* we were doing was wrong was a
very great step. It seemed to question not only our own practice, but also
that basis of trust in the exponents of our subjects under whom we had
trained. Much easier, then, to deal with the unease by attributing it either to
our own incompetence or to motivational factors in the children. Easier to
believe that *how* we were doing it rather than *what* we were doing was
wrong. It was for this reason that it became clear that it was essential to
work at the problem according to the methods of the scientist—in short, to
contribute to the science of science-teaching.

The process of scientific discovery, almost by definition, means changing
the view of things which one has received. The more we studied the different aspects of science education reported in Chapter 3 to 10, the more we
had to give up the notion that we had a simple key to the curriculum-
modification process. The virtues of the heuristic approach, which once we
had believed so valuable, appeared at last a device by which the cognitive stage
of only the top 5 per cent of thirteen year-olds could be utilised in the learning process. For the rest it would be manifestly wrong and dismotivating.

Another assumption which had to go is that what is 'sweet'[1] to the high-level teacher must be right for the pupil. To get, in the school context, closer and closer to the actual thinking and experimental processes of the university scientist may seem not only joy but manifestly *right* to many a science teacher. Yet in the light of the way in which pupils interpret our curricula this assumption appears to be a self-indulgence on the part of the teacher who satisfied himself and a few pupils at the expense of most of his pupils. Unless and until such assumptions are recognised, and laid to rest, the process of ever-increasing cognitive demand of science curricula is likely to continue.

NOTE

1 Oppenheimer's phrase to describe the attraction of the physics which caused physicists to work on the Hydrogen Bomb project in spite of their thoughts about the political consequences.

12 Strategies for improving the match

So far the discussion on the implications of the research results presented in this book has been rather negative, concentrating on examples of mismatch. The underlying implication is that science education in schools could be significantly improved if steps were taken to improve the match between the lesson material and the cognitive level of the pupil. In this chapter some possibilities and methods for improving the match will be considered.

The process of curriculum analysis (Chapter 8), together with estimates of the pupils current levels of cognitive development (either by extrapolation from the national survey results, or more reliably by the use of Science Reasoning Tasks) will allow the teacher to pinpoint particular areas of likely mismatch in his/her teaching curriculum. This should not be misunderstood so as to lead to a wholesale jettisoning of curriculum topics because the pupils are not ready to grasp their meaning at the most sophisticated level at which subject-specialists may wish to have them taught eventually.

In Part 3 the importance of specifying the various objectives inherent in a topic was stressed. This can aid the curriculum developer, or the teacher faced with planning the next few weeks work, in at least three ways:

1 One may realise that the implicit objective of a topic is inappropriate for the pupil. In this case the action indicated, of course, would be to find alternative objectives that *were* suitable.

2 The breakdown of a topic into objectives may lead to a description of many different levels at which the pupil may attribute meaning to the topic, and hence the differing depths to which it can be taught. This was the use to which the Leeds teachers put the Heat study featured in

Chapter 6. Such a clarification of objectives should enable the teacher to anticipate likely difficulties, and in the case of a topic with rather wide aims, such as Evolution, could lead to a good working hypothesis about where in the pupils' school career it would be most profitable to introduce the various sub-objectives. Alternatively it may lead one to realise that the depth at which the pupil is likely to interpret the activity would make it inappropriate for *that* objective, but sufficient for another.

3 Such analysis can lead to the successful choice of an approach to a topic, where an alternative set of objectives are shown to make conceptual demands which make it impossible for a particular group of pupils to achieve understanding. One example is reaction kinetics in chemistry and biology, where the traditional approach through rate equations constitutes a 'high energy barrier' for most pupils. In this particular case a perfectly valid level of understanding can be reached at the late concrete level simply by arranging to keep the volume of the system constant while one reagent is doubled in quantity. The consequent doubling of the reaction rate will generalise easily at that level to a principle of speed increasing linearly with the amount of reagent. Such an understanding in a pupil with no system of chemical concepts may be of limited value in chemistry, but a significant aid to understanding some concepts in biology.

Mixed ability classes

We have so far discussed possible strategies for matching as if the teacher was faced with a homogeneous group of pupils—as if the whole of one class operated at the late concrete stage while the whole of another could be relied upon to use formal operational thinking when needed. Amongst comprehensive schools, only in a large one (say 8 form entry) which operated a strict and often reviewed streaming policy would this even approximate to the truth. The real situation is probably that most first forms, and an increasing number of second and third years, are either only loosely 'setted' or have no internal streaming by ability at all. What this means in terms of the range of ability in a class is shown in Table 12.1, which gives the approximate number of pupils at each stage of cognitive development in an 'average' class of 30 pupils, at different ages, assuming random distribution and a truly comprehensive intake to the school.

Although it has been suggested that in general the slightly below average do better in mixed-ability classes than where strict streaming is operated,

Table 12.1 Range of ability in an 'average' class.

		11 +	13 +	15 +
	Age			
	Form	1	3	5
Stage	Grade	6	8	10
<2A		2	0.5	0
2A & 2A/B		15	7	3
2B & 2B/3A		11	17	17
3A		2	4	6
3B		0	1.5	4

and that the above-average do less well [45], the problems seem more acute in the case of science. When one remembers the qualitative differences in childrens' thinking at the different stages one can appreciate the real difficulty of providing a science curriculum for such a group. There is no question of finding a 'right' level which is both comprehensible to the early concrete child, and of some value to the early formal ones, especially if the curriculum is structured so that its concepts are integrated by formal modelling.

In a curriculum adaptation procedure described by Tony Ireland [22], the aims of a first-year (11+) Physical Science course were retained, but sets of alternative learning sequences were written with the intention of allowing each pupil to reach his/her maximum potential. Individual learning materials accessible to an early concrete, late concrete, and early formal level were prepared, and assigned to pupils according to their performance on two Science Reasoning Tasks. For the topic of Elements, found particularly difficult by pupils, the attainment of the aims by a four-form entry year using the adapted materials was compared with the performance of a previous year, on the same examination written specifically to test understanding. The previous year had been taught the same topics on a whole-class basis, despite the fact that each was a mixed-ability class. The experimental year retained the same organisation for practicals and information lessons, but used the work-sheets where the lesson-material emphasised concepts.

The pupils with a mean performance of 2B on the SRTs had a 31.7 per cent success-rate on exam items testing 2B objectives, compared with a success-rate of only 14.7 per cent on the same items by the pupils of the previous year taught as a whole class. For those pupils assessed at 2B/3A or or above on the SRTs from the experimental year, the success-rate on 3A exam items was 63.6 per cent, as compared with 42.8 per cent from the previous year. Thus although the performance of the pupils was not equalised, the cognitive level-matching strategy had led to an increase in the attainment of *all* pupils on objectives potentially within their understanding.

It seems inescapable to us that if the aims of high level courses, such as Nuffield O level, are to be retained, then some form of independent learning is the only way that will allow the top 15 per cent in mixed ability classes to be given a chance to proceed towards those aims. It is clear from Table 11.1 that the technique of whole-class teaching is bound to be unsatisfactory for mixed ability classes, and increasingly so as the pupils get older.

This was realised as early as 1969 by the team who designed the *Australian Science Education Project* (ASEP) [2]. Australian high schools normally have unstreamed classes, so all of the ASEP materials are modular, each of around 10 hours work for small groups (2–6 pupils). Each module is graded by Piagetian level, stage one modules demanding 2B thinking, stage two 3A thinking, and stage three 3A to 3B thinking. At least in principle it is possible for a science department to plan a multi-branched course to suit all pupils.

A similar evolution of the *Scottish Integrated Science* course has taken place in response to demand from teachers and pupils' experiences. Around a 'bead-string' of topics attempted by all pupils are higher level and lower level alternative routes, with the latter concentrating on consolidation exercises by the pupils on topics in the common course with which they have difficulty. *Insights to Science*, developed by London teachers, uses a similar structure.

In spite of shoestring funding, *Independent Learning in Science* (ILIS) has acted for some years now as a useful clearing house and proponent of the idea that mixed-ability classes in science need new techniques of classroom and laboratory organisation if the learning experience of each pupil is to be satisfactory.

It may be necessary to emphasise again that we are not concerned *only* with providing learning material suitable for the majority of pupils, using concrete operations. If there are three children capable of using formal operations in a class of thirty, then curriculum material carefully selected to make no more than concrete demands will deny mental food essential to the cognitive nourishment and further growth of those three. It has been recognised for a long time that the more able North American high school student is under-stimulated, but in Britain the problem is more recent in origin. It arises from the abolition, now almost complete, of the 11 + selection test, and from the growing belief that the streaming of pupils into classes of different ability, at least in the first few years of secondary school, is socially indefensible. There are, of course, many who believe that the most able 10 or 15 per cent of our pupils can be taken further towards the 'current network of received truths and connections' of the university practitioner, especially in specialist fields such as mathematics and the sciences, if they receive their secondary education separated from the majority. There is plenty of justification for such a belief, if one restricts ones concern to the academic domain alone, but questions of streaming and selection cannot be so restricted. They are predominantly social and political by their very nature, rather than psychological. Neither the empirical evidence we provide here, nor any other that might be obtained, could of itself determine which of two or three school systems was 'best' in any absolute sense. Criteria for judging 'better than' or 'worse than' are based on preferred views of the society. The model described in this book merely provides an explanation of the problem, and indicates some of the practical difficulties which follow from taking the mixed ability creed to its limit. One may accept that mixed ability teaching may bring social, and eventually educational advantages, but it would be foolish to underestimate the real difficulties facing the teacher, given average facilities, in trying to reap these advantages.

Cognitive acceleration: a valid alternative to matching?

In seeking ways of improving the match between learning materials and the pupil, we have so far concentrated only on the former. Logically it is proper to consider also the possibility of modifying the learner—of influencing the cognitive development of children so that they would become capable of using the high level material that we think it necessary to teach.

This raises the question of exactly what one is doing as a teacher. Is the teaching level tempered year by year to the cognitive growth of the child, or does the teaching actually cause cognitive development? This is a question of particular relevance to science teachers since so many science curricula include something like 'the development of logical thinking' in their objectives. Indeed it is one of the major justifications put forward for teaching science to all that it does promote logical thinking and the ability to assess evidence in a way that no other subject can. Anyone who has tried to implement a modern discovery-based science curriculum in place of a more formal one, or of no science at all, could have used this argument and sincerely believed in it while doing so.

Let us be clear just what is at issue here. It is whether or not different types of schooling in general, or of science teaching in particular, can actually influence the rate at which children's cognitive power develops. If one takes an extreme case, such as the difference between children of the Wolof tribe in Senegal who go to some school, and those who go to none, the answer appears to be that schooling has a significant positive effect on the rate of cognitive growth (14, but see also 25, 6, and 29). But this result might be explained in terms of 'acculturation', the familiarity of the schooled children with the strange ways of teachers and testers and the paraphernalia of education. When one looks in finer detail for the differences between the effect of different school types on rate of cognitive development, the evidence does not allow us to draw such conclusions. Results from the national survey described in Chapters 2 and 5 showed that, given due allowance for selection and for 'creaming', the proportion of children in second and third years who showed early formal thinking was the same in a great variety of schools. It appears that the rate of cognitive developemnt depended very little on the particular school environment.

More particularly, there have been many attempts to design courses or to provide interventions in the normal school programme specifically for the purpose of producing cognitive acceleration. Perhaps the most promising of these short duration acceleration studies are those of Doreen Rosenthal in Australia [44] and Deanna Kuhn in the U.S. [26]. Both studies were conducted with above average children, the first with 12 year-olds and the second with 10/11 year-olds. The first reported gains on the pendulum task sustained after two months, as a result of training on control of variables in the context of science investigations. The second merely provided problems in which variables combined in different ways were the clue to their mode of solution. The only help the children received was in being allowed to talk through what they were doing with their teacher. Again, the children showed modest gains on two Piagetian tasks, which were sustained after a period of four months. It can be argued that for above-average children this is the most likely age for rapid cognitive growth, and our view of these and the other acceleration studies reported in the literature is that, as yet, no-one has demonstrated that substantial and irreversible gains in cognitive development have been achieved as a result of science teaching deliberately designed to produce such gains.

One should distinguish here between the development of new schemas, such as occurs in the transition from concrete to formal operations, and the type of 'within stage' working out of existing schemas. The development of concrete operational thinking, from early (2A) to late (2B) consists not so much in the acquiring of new schemas as in learning to apply those partially acquired early on more and more consistently, and over a wider range of reality. For instance, in the study of heat discussed in Chapter 6, it was noticeable that a substantial proportion of the children lagged behind in their development of heat concepts what they might have been expected to achieve from their general level of development. This suggested certain lessons and experiments by which the pupils could realise their potential in this area. Here it is not so much a matter of waiting until the pupil is ready, but rather, with insight, assisting natural development.

There is further evidence which hints rather frustratingly at the futility of trying to push the rate of cognitive growth beyond certain physiologically determined limits. Herman Epstein is a brain physiologist who has collected evidence showing that in humans and mammals generally there are critical brain growth periods which are genetically programmed independently of other aspects of development such as physical adolescence [11]. In humans there are brain-growth spurts around eleven and fifteen years of age and a quiescent phase centered around thirteen. In girls the earlier spurt is more marked, in boys the later. These two brain growth phases correspond to the periods of maximum rate of development of concrete and formal operational thinking (see Figure 2.1, p. 9).

In two studies [33; 59] it was found that no evidence of formal thinking

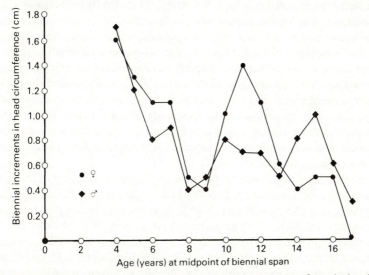

Fig. 12.1 Biennial increments in human head circumference taken from the longitudinal Berkeley Growth study. (Data from Eichhorn and Bayley 1962.)

capacity could be found in children under the age of 10, no matter how clever they were. Simple extrapolation of data relating the age of development of formal operations to IQ would suggest that children with IQs of 160 would have developed formal operational thinking by the age of 8, but this evidence suggests that the future high-level thinker is distinguished only partly by premature development, but more significantly by the rate at which he/she develops once the brain is ready. The implication of this evidence, and that of brain growth patterns, is that there is a natural limit to the extent to which one might effect a change in developmental patterns.

It will be clear that in this section we are getting perilously close to the notorious bog of the nature/nurture arguments. We propose to tiptoe around this bog, since none of our work has been directly concerned with the quality of the pupils' environment in the broadest sense to include child rearing practices and socio-cultural effects. The relation of these to subsequent cognitive growth rates is the subject of many cross-cultural Piagetian studies, but is beyond the scope of this book. The interested reader is referred to Dasen [8], and in particular to a paper in that collection by Kirk.

Returning to the narrow question of the effect of schooling on cognitive growth, the arguments and generally negative evidence presented above may be rather depressing to the science educator. Indeed, some American colleagues see the attainment of formal operational thinking by every citizen as an essential goal for a democracy, where the issues before an electorate are complex and require quite sophisticated 'if . . . . then' modelling. Whatever may be our own social and political predilections, the science of science teaching must make clear the distinction between wishful thinking and the conclusions that may properly be drawn from the evidence available. Our own view is that until definite evidence is obtained of the possibility of cognitive acceleration and the limits of its scope, the most substantial possibility of improving the experience of science teaching for most pupils lies in the cognitive level matching policy. We would argue also that the exercise of a competency is the most likely way in which its scope could most naturally increase.

Nevertheless, faced with a body of evidence which is largely of the type 'no one has yet successfully demonstrated . . . ', one is quite free to continue investigating the possibilities. If short-term training techniques have the promise that some of their authors have argued, it is obvious that a sustained use of them over a period of, say, two years could effect a radical change in the developmental patterns presented in Chapter 2. In particular, the distinction between cognitive development and the increase in a pupil's scientific knowledge and skills gained in concepts which are within his/

her capacity needs to be tested. One of the authors (MS) is already working on a research grant provided by the SSRC [5] for preliminary studies towards the design and monitoring of a two-year intervention study programme. We believe that testing the potential of such an intervention to its limit is an invstigation of great importance.

In concluding this chapter, we should raise briefly the possible implications in the population as a whole, of the current (and possibly inevitable) failure of the school system to raise more than 30 per cent of 16 year-olds to the level of formal operations, and of the apparent levelling off in cognitive growth in the year or two before this. We do not know, of course, to what extent further education—in the broadest sense to include apprenticeship, on-the-job training, or even the general experience of the 'real world' outside school—can stimulate further cognitive development. But several surveys carried out on American college students suggest that there may be little, if any further development after the age of sixteen. Deanna Kuhn has shown [27], by taking random samples of women shopping in supermarkets (in good residential districts), that the proportion utilising even early formal thinking in estimating value for money of goods offered is of the same order (30 per cent) as that found in the developmental survey for sixteen year-olds. Yet most of us, most of the time, use concrete operational thinking or less in the everyday conduct of our lives. The question can then be asked, Why does the ability to use formal operational thinking matter? We can offer two answers. The first is that the human species, as has been indicated earlier in the chapter, does have brain-growth spurts which seem programmed to make possible this level of thinking in early adolescence. The second is that formal thinking is required for most professional occupations, as well as for insight into any of the established disciplines of science and mathematics. It is also involved in any reflective process by which we distance ourselves from our everyday habits or compulsions and ask ourselves the question: Do they need be what they are? Putting these two answers together leads to a concern about the meaning of the fact that nearly 70 per cent of human beings seem not to develop a capacity which, on the face of it, they have been born to.

13 The New Science Curriculum

In Chapter 11 we described the extent of the mismatch between curriculum and pupils, and explored an hypothesis akin to natural selection to explain the increasing specialisation and rise in cognitive demand of the science curricula of the last decade. The first step away from a conditioning process of this kind is to recognise that it exists; the second is to break free from it intellectually. In looking ahead to the possible shape of science curricula of the late 80s and 90s, it will be necessary to consider not only the constraints imposed by cognitive matching, but to include also the other educational and social elements which must be taken into account if there is to be a major shift in the current paradigm of science education.

The system of selection common in Britain until a few years ago had obvious implications for the description of society as a whole. It is generally held that while Britain's strength lies in the excellence of its very highly-trained people—civil servants, university scientists, and other intellectuals, its related weakness is in the middle range of trained worker and technician and in their utilisation by industry. Yet such a bias would inevitably be produced by an educational system which has concentrated so much of its resources on the top 15 per cent or so of its population. The effect of the abolition of selection at 11 + has not yet been reflected in the system of science education in use in most schools. In *Alternatives for Science Education* [1], an important consultative document intended as a basis for discussion by the science education profession on future policy directions, it is argued that we cannot afford such a system on social grounds:

...school science has, both overtly and covertly, become more pure, conceptually demanding and complex, and less concerned with the everyday reality and experience of our youngsters, their parents and their employers: it has, in so many ways, become a complex symbolic system accessible to the few, and we do not believe that there is anything intrinsic in science, or science studies, that necessarily forces our subject in this direction. (1, p. 52)

Such arguments can be complemented by the evidence presented in this book which suggests that because of poor cognitive matching the true potential of most pupils is not being fully stimulated and realised. To the authors the latter seems even more important than the former reason, although they are obviously related.

Remaining for a little longer within the cognitive matching model, let us imagine the slate wiped clean, and ask what would even the university scientists themselves have advised on the scope of science in the comprehensive school, given the evidence presented in this book. We do not believe that they would choose the system we have inherited. Had the developmental curves of Figure 2.1 been compared with the subject-specific Tables 9.1, 9.2, and 9.3 the bright idea *might* have occurred, 'My goodness, we could get about 15 per cent of them up to here by the age of sixteen, and even 5 per cent there by fourteen'. But the sobering counter-idea must have prevailed that this could only be done at the expense of producing an elite caste separated by a wide gulf of different experience at the most formative age from the rest of the population while at school and remaining so as adults. Indeed it is obvious that if subject-specialist science requires for its proper understanding the late formal thinking which the Nuffield O and A level courses involve then it would be better to introduce it at the age when the maximum development of most people has occurred—that is, at 16 years of age. Had they reached this point, and then gone on to ask what kind of experience of science it would be desirable for all pupils to have had before the age of sixteen they may well have produced something like the models proposed in *Alternatives*. Yet even the latter is deficient without a model of the pupil population as is provided here.

Nothing so crude is suggested as that *no* thinking other than that which is concrete operational should be utilised. But with the primrose path of a neat specialist course automatically rejecting 70 per cent of the population beckoning (and being resisted!) it is suggested that the content and processes of science are inspected afresh, for those that are accessible 'in some recognisable form' (p. 99) to concrete operational thinking. These will be the major integrating experiences to be shared by all pupils. How to permit the faster developer to obtain access at a deeper level while retaining a common basis of communication is a challenge to be met (and while *he* may prefer a symbolic and intuitive mode of exploration, *she* may use a more sophisticated verbal mode). What might these experiences and processes be? How can they be evaluated? In the answers to these questions will lie the nature of the New Science Curriculum.

In effect we are questioning the model which says that the network of received truths and relationships by which the professional scientist sees the phenomena to which his science currently addresses itself should be taken as the basis of an apprenticeship sequence. We are suggesting that this is merely *one* model for possible school use, and asking for a quite different model to be considered that may, in the long run, be better even for the future science specialist.

Before trying to outline some of the major features that we envisage for this curriculum, we should try to lay to rest a line of criticism to which we have been subjected by socially aware educators. This criticism is concerned with the 'labelling' of children that is involved in describing one as using mainly concrete operations, while another has available formal operational thinking. One could be playful, and point out that, even for Engels, freedom is merely the ability to *choose* necessity. In fact there seems to be no more grounds for objecting to Piaget's work because of its determinist picture of human mental capacity than to object to the science of physiology for similar reasons. The ability to describe and estimate a person's present mental capacity is no more an instrument for maintaining the person at that level than is our ability to describe a bodily state in physiological terms. Indeed, both increase our capacity to intervene in what is the present described condition.

The view that the 'labelling' of children leads teachers to take action which confirms potential differences is not only misconceived, but itself leads to the consequences of which it accuses the approach that it opposes. If you treat a mixed-ability class as if they were all able to understand something which you think is important for them to understand, then you will force those who cannot understand to define themselves as incompetent. You treat each individual as a machine if you treat him exactly the same as all the others in the class, and thus you decrease his freedom. Our view is that by understanding the difficulties of different learners, and taking that understanding into your thinking about lesson planning you not only show respect for them as persons, but also very much increase the rate at which they are able to learn and the breadth of knowledge and skills that they can achieve. We do not deny that knowledge *can* be used to keep people 'as they are', but this can never have been good grounds in itself for not extending knowledge.

Social and political considerations

So far, our concentration on levels of cognitive development might have given the impression that we believe this to be the only important consideration in the modification of curricula or in the planning of new ones. We do believe that the cognitive demand level acts as a critically limiting constraint on the selection of objectives, but it is very far from being the only factor needed to define the curriculum. Looming large in the background of such intellectual factors are those social, and to some extent political, considerations which provide the raw material for those common room arguments about selection, streaming, and the nature of comprehensive education. Decisions reached on the basis of intellectual factors alone are sterile if they are not set realistically in the current social context.

The authors of *Alternatives* point out, quite rightly, that it is impossible to dissociate an intellectual step in curriculum reform from a social/political one. It is thus necessary for us to make an avowal here: our position is that of a democratic belief in the absolute value of each person and their equality as citizens. It would be quite possible to *choose* an elitist system of education, but we do not choose it. Nor do the authors of *Alternatives*, but in spite of their call for 'open discussion of purposes' (p. 19) they are not quite so ready to make an open avowal of their positions. Nowhere is the Marxist origin of many of their arguments credited, and we think the document is the weaker for that.

Its strength, however, lies in the descriptive analysis given of all present curriculum schemas, whether orthodox or experimental, and in a set of three proposals for change which might follow from this proposition:

> ...the primary justification, and therefore purpose, of science education is to foster and develop, as part of the general education of the individual, a scientific way of thinking, a basic knowledge of scientific ideas and an ability to communicate with others.

We are broadly in agreement with the spirit which lies behind these proposals (pp. 37–54) and believe that a constructive resonse to them on the part of all those concerned with science education is of vital importance to pupils. Therefore the rest of this book will be concerned with the relevance of the model presented to what might be a science curriculum accessible to all. This 'all' must include both the minority who were catered for in the 60s by the Nuffield projects in Britain, and PSSC, Chemstudy, and BSCS in America, and the great majority which those projects (with the honourable exception of Nuffield Secondary Science) ignored. The profession is really again in a situation as if there was no science tradition, and one needed to be invented. What can be done is to set the ground rules.

We shall make a start by considering:

The mathematics connection

The professional physicist or chemist tends to take a predatory view of mathematics as a servant or a tool. In Chapter 9 it was suggested that O (and hence A) level physics was largely the growth of a particular kind of mathematical modelling of the world. Physical chemistry requires a similar skill. It comes as something of a surprise, then, to encounter the apparent disdain of the mathematics teacher for the (to him or her) unnecessary physical embodiment of mathematical relationships and operations. The mathematics used in the physical sciences is but a small corner relating to computation, algebraic manipulations, and elementary calculus.

If the 2B columns of taxonomy 1 and 2 are scanned it will be seen at once that there is a natural limit to the extent to which an early secondary school child can appreciate the mathematician's view that the test of a mathematical operation or system is self-consistency and provability, rather than any empirical reality test. The luxury of the distinction is plainly one which only a person with access to late formal operational thinking could afford (e.g. taxonomy 1.2; taxonomy 2.4). At any earlier stage of development the mathematical system will not effectively be dissociated from its physical embodiment. Many mathematicians who have concerned themselves with the development of the 'new mathematics' for primary and early secondary schools have readily accepted that mathematical relationships can only be modelled in physical reality [38].

Among the less welcome findings of our CSMS mathematics colleagues [7] was the fact that, in applying several mathematics operations to reality many comprehensive school pupils are *less* competent after four years in secondary education than they were at the outset. Now the physical embodiment in which middle and early secondary school pupils require to find mathematical concepts is in many cases the subject matter of science. Psychologically there is no justification for teaching these subjects separately until the pupils are at a stage of cognitive development advanced enough to allow them to operate differently in the two fields.

The operations of the number scale are naturally embodied in what are called the 'conservations', and scales such as those of temperature, acidity (pH), and voltage, as well as length itself. Competence in these operations is usually taken for granted by the teacher of secondary science, but those who have questioned this and given courses explicitly designed to enrich experience of quantitative physical relationships have been rewarded by rapid advances in understanding by their pupils. For example, a group of pupils in a Bedfordshire middle school were found to be about one year below average by SRT II, Volume and Heaviness. They were then given six weeks of 'remedial' teaching which concentrated on measurement procedures and the use of scales. Six months later the same SRT indicated that they were now a little above average in levels of cognitive development. This is another example of the apparent acceleration of cognitive development *within* the concrete operational stage.

The other area of natural overlap between mathematics and science activity for pupils in the 10 to 13 year-old range forms a well-established part of 'New Maths' courses. What in mathematics is the connection between a set theory approach to number and various kinds of graphical representation, is in biology (and in social sciences) the concepts of range and average, of variation, and of elementary sampling to tell whether a change in a community has really taken place. Use of 'distribution boards' or a similar device occurs in physics, biology, and mathematics courses, each largely in ignorance of the other's activities. If one mark of science is the 'mathematicisation' of reality, then elementary statistics are far more fundamental to science than the algebraic transformations applied often mindlessly in physics and chemistry higher up the school. If one thinks of the use of scientific method in political and industrial life these basic concepts relating to the handling of evidence are of far more importance to far more people than the manipulative competence which is required of the future specialist or high-level technician. Again, the notions of correlation, probability, and error are conspicuously absent from the traditional 'games' described in Chapter 9.

A spectrum of the sciences

In our search for the ground rules of the New Science Curriculum, we will turn now from the mathematics connection to the range of sciences that might possibly be seen as sources of activities. These can be placed on a spectrum according to the different ways in which they employ 'a scientific way of thinking':

'Hard' .... 'Soft'
Physics   Chemistry   Biology   Psychology   Sociology   Anthropology
  Astronomy   Geology   Meteorology

There is almost a complete divide across the middle of the spectrum between the conceptual methods, with their associated aspects of mathematics. Here is a comparative list of some of the methods used:

(a) *The 'hard' sciences*
Measurement
Precision
Functional relationships (1:1, or 3 or 4 variables at the most with a strict relationship
Deductive models tightly related to the data they explain (e.g. kinetic theory; electrons)

(b) *Social sciences and biology*
Mean values
Variation
Correlation relationships
Interaction between variables
Questionnaires
Interviews
Problem of subjective bias
Sampling, and generalisation from a sample

The first tends to produce models that are atomistic and analytic: the second tends to holistic models.

Traditional school science has drawn heavily from the left-hand list, and very little from the right. Yet, as was pointed out in the discussion of the mathematics connection all the methods in the right-hand list have a valid realisation 'in some recognisable form' accessible to concrete thinking. They are also capable of great sophistication without contradicting the insight obtainable by concrete thinking. Therefore on grounds of cognitive development alone there is a strong case for some new curriculum invention being drawn from the softer side of the spectrum.

There are three other good reasons for choosing activities and content from the 'soft' side.

(a) It offers the opportunity for a connection with mathematics to the benefit of both, and at a lower level than do the 'hard' sciences.
(b) The subject-matter of the social sciences and biology offers an approach to scientific thinking more in accord with the personal interests of most young girls [24], and of those boys who at present choose against studying traditional sciences as soon as they can.
(c) —related to (b). The methods of the social sciences relate scientific thinking more obviously to the issues of everyday life than do the hard sciences. To the future citizen this is a more direct reason for their study.

A strong argument, on social grounds, is made in *Alternatives for Science Education* for Environmental Science as the main activity for the first two years of secondary education. As in the ASE pamphlet *Science for the Under-Thirteens* emphasis is laid on finding science explorations which arise out of the spontaneous interests of the children. Some of the methods by which this could be realised will come from the traditional sciences, but many will need to be drawn from the social sciences.

The personality connection

An aspect of the CSMS research not discussed in this book is that of personality development. Only if the aims and content of science are related to a model of how the child proceeds through adolescence to crystallise an adult personality is it at all likely that the pupil will be well-motivated toward the content and processes of science which our curricula offer. This is particularly a problem in the middle school and the first three years of secondary education, when the attitudes of pupils become formed and affect decisions they will make about further study of science. Many of our established routines in physical sciences are ill-matched to the interests of girls of twelve and thirteen years of age, for example. Work by John Head using a model of ego-development, and leading to a model of psycho-sexual development predictive of attitudes of boys and girls to different science activities at different ages [17] should be a valuable component to the cognitive development model in curriculum development in the Eighties.

We see, then, that the New Science Curriculum is likely to be characterised by:

(a) its suitability for the great majority of pupils in comprehensive schools;

(b) its coordination, if not integration, with a New Mathematics Curriculum;

(c) the addition of much material taken from the softer end of the scale of sciences;

(d) its recognition of both the affective and cognitive needs of pupils.

A brief look at some existing courses which display some of these characteristics will exemplify the point we are making here, and provide sources of 'form' for discussion.

MAN: A COURSE OF STUDY (MACOS) [34]

It may seem surprising that Jerome Bruner was one of the most strenuous advocates of the cognitive level matching policy argued for in this book.

Indeed, the real meaning of the famous phrase about 'any learner' is that it is only by considering the logical power of the learner that 'any body of knowledge' can in some sense be made accessible to him. It was for this reason that he was so closely associated with the development of 'Modern Maths' teaching. With the hindsight of the research presented in this book it is possible to see that much of the curriculum development work which originated around him in the late Fifties and early Sixties was deficient only in that it lacked one half of the match—that of a developmental model of the whole population of child-learners. By concentrating research and development work on very intelligent children the seed was sown of the eventual backlash against the new approach to school education. 'It seems quite reasonable', he said [3, p. 57], 'to suppose that the thought processes that were going on in the children are quite ordinary among eight-year-old human beings'—this, after admitting that they were in the IQ-range 120–130 in a private school and from high-level professional homes, presumably in the Harvard area. The methods of MACOS contain many of the answers we are going to need. Its subject-matter lies well over to the 'softer' end of the spectrum of the sciences—the fields of anthropology, sociology, and zoology. How can one make children, each at his/her own level, aware of themselves in relation to his own society in contrast to that of the Eskimo, bushmen, and primates? What is the function of child-rearing practices? These questions are as much part of the scope of science as those relating to energy in physics or structure and function in biology. More important, following the picture we have sketched of the lack of match between the cognitive development of children and the expectations of science courses, and the fact that for the majority of secondary school pupils concrete thinking will be their predominant way of structuring information, the methods developed by this pioneering course will repay close study and informed reporting. In designing the course originally for 10 year-olds, its originators had to find, by both trial and error and theory, what methods of study would enable concrete thinkers to find their own meaning in comparisons of behaviour which normally only form part of the complex conceptual apparatus of the adult research specialist. Bruner provided the theory of operating in the ikonic or concrete mode. This, we have argued, is precisely the new problem which faces us with respect to physics, chemistry, and biology subject-matter.

An additional reason for the close study of 'the form' of MACOS lies in its classroom methods. If the natural way in to scientific thinking for most 11–14 year-olds is through social-science subject matter, then experience in the practise of its pupil-centred discussion methods (perhaps particularly congenial to girls) would be an essential part of the re-training of teachers learning new 'games'.

SCIENCE 5–13 AND MATCH AND MISMATCH

Science 5–13 [46], with the later *Match and Mismatch* [16] training schemes developed by Wynne Harlen for helping the teacher both to follow the progress of her pupils and assist their learning, is another and different source of 'form'. The spirit of the source-books comes from that movement in primary school education which stresses starting from the spontaneous interests of children. If the ASE recommendations for middle and early secondary school science are to be realised, this is a valuable mine of possible activities. However as the books stand they do not give much help to the secondary school teacher, or the teacher in the middle schools which have secondary school timetables. It is for this reason that the evaluation of *Structure and Forces* and *Ourselves*, mentioned in Chapter 6, was initiated. The teacher needs an interpretative 'map' of the possible interconnections between activities if he is to plan for the arrival of twenty to thirty pupils two or three times a week in his classroom or laboratory. As with MACOS, we need reported case-studies of this approach in action in our schools.

Both the ASEP modules [2] and the *Science Curriculum Improvement Study* (SCIS) [47] course have been discussed in some detail by one of the authors elsewhere [13]. The former are notable both for a possible solution to the mixed-ability class problem and also because some of them show how to organise some social science studies at the concrete, early formal, and late formal level in as detailed a manner as does NCS for traditional sciences. SCIS would certainly repay transplanting from the American to the British context for evaluative study. In contrast to *Science 5–13*, and in spite of being designed for the 7 to 12 year-old, the SCIS course is highly structured. Amongst many other good routines, or 'games', are exercises by which concepts such as 'Interaction' and 'Frame of Reference' can be realised at the 2A, 2B, and 3A levels.

It is clear that if a major change in our paradigm of school science activity is to take place, the same kind of economy of effort as is practised in good industrial research and development needs to become as much an obvious way of using our resources as the monolithic headquarters team seemed to be in the sixties. In this we concur exactly with recommendation five [1, p. 53] of *Alternatives for Science Education*:

... we recommend that substantial resources be allocated to a major programme of research and development that seeks to evaluate alternative definitions of school science.

...and which develops a series of small-scale and intensive studies of the nature of young people's conceptualisations of science and scientific processes.

Into practice

It can be seen that the New Science Curriculum might have a very different face from that which the majority of science teachers have been used to. Yet a going system, a 'machine', can only change when a valid alternative has not only been tested and found feasible, but can be successfully 'taught' or communicated to teachers so that they can practice it with confidence.

It would be out of place in a book reporting research results to dwell at length on the logistics of implementation of a new curriculum, but we cannot conclude without at least recognising three areas in need of attention: communication, the published materials, and teacher re-education.

COMMUNICATION

In the quieter days of the twenties, routines of teaching became transmitted and established by teachers writing textbooks containing their own solutions. Those which could be used successfully elsewhere sold, and those which were too idiosyncratic did not. In this way a tradition of science teaching was established, and the *School Science Review* became a useful forum for the transmission of ideas within a commonly held framework of ideas in science education. How could a New Science Curriculum become established as a known competence among science teachers?

The Sixties answer to this question, both in Britain and the United States, was the large headquarters team. The Eighties method does not yet have a recognisable face but the signs are that it will be decentralised, even democratic in the sense that the experiences and imagination of many different workers in education will be utilised. Yet we do not believe that major change will come about unless some unifying body of people with power to act are there to direct effort. If local teacher groups working towards curriculum solutions, researchers offering evaluation skills, research teachers reporting case studies, DES (Government) committees discussing a core curriculum, College and University educationists working on a philosophy of science, and many others are to produce something better than Babel, then communication will be the key.

In a book devoted to the proposition that a science of science teaching is a meaningful aim it need only be said that this communication problem is exactly that of the major branches of science, and that it is one of the marks of science that it does get solved. It seems to us that the science teachers' associations (in Britain, the ASE) might take the key role by developing and extending the part they already play in providing a meeting point for all of the interested parties. In this connection the recent publication of *What is Science?* [60], in which the various views of current philosophers of science are explained for science teachers can be seen as the ASE already fulfilling part of this function.

MATERIALS

The extent to which a new curriculum will be adopted by the profession depends heavily on the nature of the printed and other materials that define it. For example, notwithstanding the evidence presented here of the unsuitability of Nuffield Combined Science for the majority of pupils, it is by far the most popular science curriculum in use in its age range in England and Wales. In contrast, Nuffield Secondary Science, although highly commended by science educators, appears to be relatively little used. Apart from the fact that NCS looks more like the sort of science that most teachers are used to, its popularity must be due in large measure to its excellent detailed lesson-by-lesson guides which the teacher can follow, even into areas outside his specialisation. NSS demands far more of the teacher, both in constructing a course from the resource material, and in the effort involved in arranging a mode 3^1 syllabus and examination.

This is the snag of other experimental curricula of the Sixties, such as *Science 5–13*, and even ASEP. Whatever their merits, they ask too much of the teacher by way of everyday and every month planning. In Britain, too, unless a course is in principle *examinable* at 15+ it is very difficult to establish a common mind among teachers as to what are the limits and scope of their teaching commitment. A very strong feature of the Nuffield courses was that they created new forms of examinations which tested the real course objectives. A New Science Curriculum will only come into being if the logistics of communication and the logistics of the everyday teaching life of the school science department are fine-tuned sufficiently to each other to evolve new solutions to these problems. It seems to us inescapable that in this process the DES in Britain, and the central authority in education in other countries will need to find a new role. This may be less autocratic than in the past and more scientific in the sense that it uses the methods of exploration and of testing the validity of exploration which have become part of what we recognise as the scientific method.

TEACHERS

If his initial training is through a first degree in science, and a postgraduate year of education, the teacher is shown something of the method and the value of the scientific approach. He is shown this by specialists whose judgements in relation to their specialities will always be greater than his own. Yet his task as a teacher is to do something for which his first degree training will have given him little preparation, although his education training should have set his feet in the right direction. On the one hand he has to learn to see his pupils as developing persons to whom he has a primary responsibility: to give as much of what may be of value to them from science as possible. On the other hand he needs to take a view of science which is more that of a philosopher of science than of the professional scientist. This is because, like most professionals, the average scientist will need too much of his mind and energy concentrated in the practise of his science to allow him to be very reflective about what he is doing. The teacher will almost daily be confronted with questions from his pupils both about the value of what he is teaching, and about the particular 'rules' which it embodies which makes it different from other school activities. From this it follows that the intellectual activity which will be required is not only that of his first degree discipline, but also will be that of participating in the impact and change of science in the world at large, which we have described as philosophical.

Moreover, with the growth of integrated science teaching at the junior secondary level it is much rarer than it was for a teacher to be able to teach exclusively in his own special subject area. Thus whereas the university scientist can rarely afford to think in terms other than his own discipline, the science teacher must always be thinking of what there is in common with all three of the major traditional sciences, and how they are each different facets of 'science'. Only in this way can he create learning experiences for his pupils which are both meaningful to them and recognisable to the scientist as scientific in spirit and content.

We believe that there is now a new intellectual challenge in front of the science teacher—even for the teacher who wishes to keep his mind alive in the specialist discipline to which he has been initiated. We hope that this book has sketched a part of this challenge.

NOTE

* Mode 3 Certificate of Secondary Education is an examination system in which the school sets its own syllabus and examinations, which may include an element of assessment of course work. A sample of pupils' assessments are moderated by an external examination board to ensure the maintenance of national standards.

References

Background reading, which may be helpful:

(a) in the work of Piaget: Flavell, J. H. *The Developmental psychology of Jean Piaget.* Princeton: Van Nostrand

(b) in statistics: Guilford, J. P. *Fundamental statistics in psychology and education.* New York: McGraw-Hill

Quoted in text:

1 ASE (1979) *Alternatives for Science Education.* ASE, College Lane, Hatfield, Herts

2 ASEP (1974) *A Guide to ASEP.* Melbourne: Australian Science Education Project, Victoria Government Printer

3 Bruner, J. S. (1968) *Toward a theory of instruction* (Chapter 4). New York: W. W. Norton & Co. Inc

4 CHEMSTUDY (1963) *Chemistry: an experimental science.* San Francisco: Freeman

5 CASE (1980–1982) *Cognitive Acceleration through Science Education.* Two year exploratory study funded by SSRC: grant no.HR 7492, at Chelsea College. Directors: Paul Black and Michael Shayer

6 Cole, M., Gay, J., Glick, J., and Sharp, D. (1971) *The cultural context of learning and thinking.* London: Methuen

7 CSMS Mathematics Team (1980) *Children's understanding of mathematics: 11 to 16.* London: John Murray

8 Dasen, P. R. (1977) *Piagetian psychology: cross cultural contributions.* New York: Gardener Press

9 Deadman, J. A. (1976) *The structure and development of concepts associated with the topic of evolution in secondary school boys.* PhD. London

10 Eichorn, D., & Bayley, N. (1962) Growth in head circumference from birth through early adulthood. *Child Dev.* 33, 257–71

11 Epstein, H. T. (1974) Phrenoblysis: special brain and mind growth periods. I. Human Brain and Skull Development. *Developmental Psychobiology*, 7, (3), 207–16

Epstein, H. T. (1977) A neuroscience framework for restructuring middle school curricula. *Transescence*, 5, 6–11

Epstein, H. T. (1978) Growth spurts during Brain Development: Implications for Educational Policy and Practice. Chapter X in *Education and the Brain*. Chall, J. S. & Mirsky, A. F. (Eds) NSSE Yearbook. University of Chicago Press

Epstein, H. (1979) *Development and evolution of brain size*, Chap. 6 New York: Academic Press

12 Erickson, G. L. (1979) Children's conceptions of heat and temperature. *Science Education*, 63, (2), 221–30

13 Gallagher, J. Mc.C. & Easley, J. A. (eds.) (1978) Chapter 4 by K. Lovell and M. Shayer, in *Knowledge and Development*: Vol. 2, Piaget and Education. New York: Plenum

14 Greenfield, P. (1966) On culture and conservation. In Bruner, Olver, and Greenfield

15 Hallam, R. N. (1969) Piaget and the teaching of history. *Educational Research*, 12, 3–12

16 Harlen, W., et al. (1977) *Match and Mismatch: raising questions: fitting learning to development for five to thirteen year olds*. Oliver and Boyd (Edinburgh) for the Schools Council

17 Head, J. (1980) A model to link personality characteristics to a preference for science. *European J. Sci. Ed.* Vol. 3 (in preparation)

18 H.M.I. Report (1978) *Primary Education in England*. London: HMSO
    H.M.I. Report (1980) *Aspects of Secondary Education*. London: HMSO

19 I.L.I.S. *Independent Learning in Science*. Editor: D. Foster, Resources for Learning Development Unit, Redcross Street, Bristol BS2 0BA

20 Ingle, R. B. and Shayer, M. (1971) Conceptual Demands of Nuffield O-level Chemistry. *Educ. in Chem.* 8 (5), 182–3

21 Inhelder, B. and Piaget, J. (1958) *The Growth of Logical Thinking*. London: Routledge & Kegan Paul

22 Ireland, A. J. (1980) *The feasibility of matching the Piagetian stages of cognitive development of children, to the intellectual demand within a science curriculum, as an aid to curriculum development*. M.Sc. York

23 Johnson, D. (1977) *High School Mathematics and Science Concepts Profile*. Report written for Saskatoon Public Board of Education Saskatoon, Saskatchewan, Canada S7K 1M7

24 Kelly, A. (1978) *Girls and Science*. Stockholm: Almquist and Wiksell

25 Kimball, R. (1971) *Ekyetagsia Ekikulu—an enquiry into the relationship between a new science curriculum and cognitive growth*. SIDEC, Stanford University

26 Kuhn, D. and Angelev, J. (1976) An experimental study of the development of formal operational thought. *Child Development*, 47, 597–706

27 Capon N. and Kuhn D. (1979) Logical Reasoning in the Supermarket: Adult females' use of a proportional reasoning strategy in an everyday context. *Dev. Psych.* 15, 450–2

28 LAMP Project (1976): Ed. D. Wilkinson and J. Bowers. Hatfield: ASE

29 Laurendeau-Bendavid, M. (1977) *Culture, schooling and cognitive development*. in Dasen (1977)
30 Lawson, A. E., Karplus, R. and Adi, H. (1978) The acquisition of propositional logic and formal operational schemata during the secondary school years. *Journal of Research in Science Teaching* 15, 6, 465–478
31 Leeds Middle Years Science Curriculum Project (1979). Project Director: Mrs. Ann Squires. Leeds City Council, Department of Education.
32 Lovell, K. (1961) A follow-up study of Inhelder and Piaget's the Growth of Logical Thinking. *Br. J. Psychol.*, 52, 143–153
33 Lovell, K. and Shields, J. B. (1967). Some aspects of a study of the gifted child. *Br. J. educ. Psychol.* 37, 2, 201–208
34 *Man: a course of study*. In the UK, there is a National Training and Support Programme. Information can be obtained from Mrs. Lucilla Haynes, National Secretary, MACOS, CARE, University of East Anglia, Norwich NR4 7TJ
35 NFER (1979) *Science Reasoning Tasks*. NFER Publishing Co., 2 Oxford Road East, Windsor, Berks
36 *Nuffield Combined Science* Harlow, Essex: Longman
37 *Nuffield Combined Science Themes for the Middle Years* (1980) Harlow, Essex: Longman
38 *Nuffield Mathematics Project* (1970) Checking Up 1 (frontispiece and introduction). Harlow, Essex: Longman
39 *Nuffield Secondary Science*: Harlow, Essex: Longman.
40 *Nuffield Science 13–16* (1980, 1981) Harlow, Essex: Longman
41 Ormerod, M. B., & Duckworth, D. (1975) *Pupils' attitudes to science: a review of research*. Windsor: NFER
42 Peel, E. A. (1971) *The nature of adolescent judgement*. London: Staple Press
43 PSSC (1965) Physics. Boston: D. C. Heath
44 Rosenthal, D. A. (1975) *An investigation of some factors influencing development of formal operational thinking*. Ph.D. University of Melbourne
    Rosenthal, D. A. (1979) Acquisition of formal operations: the effects of two training procedures. *J. Genet. Psych.* 134, 125–40
45 Ross, J. M., et al. (1972) *A critical appraisal of comprehensive education*. Windsor: NFER
46 Science 5/13 (1972). *With Objectives in Mind*. London: Macdonald Educational
47 SCIS (1974). *Science Curriculum Improvement Study:* see SCIS Teacher's Handbook, Lawrence Hall of Science, University of California, Berkeley California 94720
48 SCISP: *Schools Council Integrated Science Project, Teacher's Handbook* (Chapter 4). Harlow, Essex: Longman
49 Shayer, M. (1972). *Piaget's work and science teaching*. M.Ed. Leicester
50 Shayer, M. (1972). Conceptual Demands in Nuffield O-level Physics. *School Sci. Rev.* 186, 54, 26–34

Shayer, M. (1974). Conceptual Demands in the Nuffield O-level Biology Course. *School Sci. Rev.* 56, 195, 381–388

51 Shayer, M., Küchemann, D. E. and Wylam, H. (1976). The distribution of Piagetian stages of thinking in British middle and secondary school children. *Br. J. educ. Psychol.*, 46, 164–173

52 Shayer, M. (1978). *A Test of the Validity of Piaget's Construct of Formal Operational thinking*. PhD. University of London

53 Shayer, M. and Wylam, H. (1978). The distribution of Piagetian stages of thinking in British middle and secondary school children. II: 14–16 year-olds and sex differentials *Br. J. educ. Psychol.* 48, 62–70

54 Shayer, M. (1978). The analysis of science curricula for Piagetian level of demand. *Studies in Science Education*, Leeds, 5, 115–130

55 Shayer, M. (1978). Nuffield Combined Science: do the pupils understand it? *School Science Review*, 60, 211, 210–223

56 Shayer, M. (1979). Has Piaget's construct of formal operational thinking any utility? *Br. J. educ. Psychol.* 49, 265–276

57 Shayer, M., Adey, P. and Wylam, H. (1980). Group Tests of Cognitive Development: Ideals and a Realisation. *J. Res. Sci. Teach.* (accepted for publication November 1979)

58 Shayer, M. and Wylam, H. (1980). The development of the concepts of heat and temperature in 10–13 year-olds. *J. Res. Sci. Teach.* (accepted for publication)

59 Webb, R. A. (1974). Concrete and Formal Operations in very bright 6 to 11 year-olds. *Hum. Dev.* 17, 292–300

60 *What is Science?* (1980). Study Series No. 15. Hatfield: ASE

Index